Mission Stories
From Around
The World

Also by J. Lawrence Driskill:

Mission Adventures in Many Lands

Japan Diary of Cross-Cultural Mission

Mission Stories From Around The World

J. Lawrence Driskill

Hope Publishing House
Pasadena, California

For information address:
Hope Publishing House
Southern California Ecumenical Council
P. O. Box 60008
Pasadena, California 91116 - U.S.A.
Telephone (818) 792-6123; FAX (818) 792-2121

Cover design - Michael McClary/The Workshop

Printed in the U.S.A. on acid-free paper.

Illustrations from *The Good News Paper* (Grades 3-4) and *Lifesigns* (Grades 5-6), *Celebrate* Curriculum. Copyright © 1991, 1992 and 1993 The Presbyterian Publishing House. Used by permission.

Library of Congress Cataloging-in-Publication Data

Driskill, J. Lawrence, 1920-
    Mission stories from around the world / J. Lawrence Driskill.
        p.   cm.
    Summary: Japan, Latin America, and Africa are the settings for some of these mission adventures.
    ISBN 0-932727-72-7 (lib. bdg.) : $19.95. -- ISBN 0-932727-71-9 (pbk.) : $11.95
    1. Christian biography--Juvenile literature. I. Title.
BR1700.2.D75 1994
266'.0092--dc20
[B]   93-39413
                                      CIP

Dedicated to our grandchildren,
Heather and Ian McCurry,
who have brightened
our senior years
with love and joy.

Acknowledgments

First I want to thank those whose stories appear here. Without their good examples of faith and service to God and God's people, I could not have written this book.

I am grateful to Dr. Christy Wilson, Dr. Dudley Woodberry, Dr. Dean Thompson and Dr. Pasquale Castellano, all of whom honored me with their words of encouragement and commendation.

I owe thanks to Ms. Osanna Love Gooding and the Westminster Gardens Writers' Group she advises for helpful suggestions. Ms. Faye Burdick kindly edited seven of the stories when they were used in the Presbyterian (USA) Celebrate curriculum.

Special thanks are due Ms. Faith Annette Sand, who took major responsibility for editing and publishing the book, and to Ms. Susan Parry for typing it into her wonder-working computer.

Seven of the illustrations are used with the permission of the Presbyterian Publishing House, which first published those stories. Some of the stories were illustrated with photographs. The remainder of the illustrations were done by Mrs. Betty Harter. I am deeply indebted to Betty for her creative contribution to the book.

Most of all, I thank God whose guidance and help brought all these things together to produce this book—a book of mission stories from around the world. May God be glorified through them.

Table of Contents

Foreword, *Dr. J. Christy Wilson, Jr.* ix

Introduction xi

1. Ariet's Search for Love 1

2. A Revolutionary Finds Peace 5

3. Danger in Africa 10

4. Genzo, a Poet of Japan 13

5. A Murderer Brings Peace 16

6. Orop's Sacrifice for a Friend 20

7. Rosita Braves the Altiplano 23

8. Francis, a Kenyan Evangelist 28

9. The Mayans' First Doctor 32

10. From Sudanese Slave to Minister 36

11. Takeo Becomes a Christian 40

12. Zia, a Blind Afghan Christian 47

13. Village of Life 51

14. Missionary Clinic at Pokwo 53

15. A Group Wedding at Doleib Hill 56

16. The Missionary Lion 59

17. Lyda, the Healer 61

18. Missionary to Quezaltenango 66

19. A Hostage in Beirut 71

20. Katie's African Escapades 77
21. A Gang Leader Turns to Christ 80
22. A Home for the Homeless 84
23. Alice Goes to Japan 87
24. A Grandma's Memories 92
25. Crystal Pioneers in California 97
26. Ted Overcomes His Problem 103
27. A Poem for Grandma 108
28. Elizabeth and Her Talking Birds 111
29. Adventures in Thailand 113
30. Helping One Another 116
31. Dr. Hail's "Almighty Turtle" 121
32. Father of the Ainu 125
33. A Challenge for Sarah 128
34. Alice Goes to Japan's Siberia 133
35. Betty Teaches Through Love 139
36. Keeping Young in Japan 142
37. Serving God in Japan 147
38. The Unwanted Child 151
39. Woman Police Helicopter Pilot 157
40. Genevieve, Content at 102 162
41. Healthy at Age 102 165
42. Serving Retired Missionaries 169
43. My Christian Grandpa 173
44. A World of Joy and Wonder 175

Foreword

In the introduction to this book, Dr. J. Lawrence Driskill refers to Jesus Christ as the "greatest story-teller of all." Since he, along with his wife Lillian, served as missionaries in Japan for many years, they have seen how important a place the art of story telling holds in Asian societies today. People all around the world love a good illustration.

Stories are so important as a means of communication that it was prophesied that the Messiah would use this method to reveal new truths. We read, "Jesus spoke all these things to the crowd in parables. ... So was fulfilled what was spoken through the prophet, 'I will open my mouth in parables, I will utter things hidden since the creation of the world' " (Mt 13:34-35).

This book, in a sense, is an extension of the ability of our Lord to illustrate truths through stories. But here it is the lives of those who demonstrated his incarnational love in their service in missions. They are a fulfillment of God's promise, "It is God who is at work in you, both to will and to do of his good pleasure" (Philippians 2:13).

I believe that the greatest inspirational reading, next to the Bible, comes from delving into the biographies of women and men who have been used of God in their time. In this volume one gets illustrations of facts about real people that prove stranger than fiction.

The greatest investment that we have is our lives. These accounts show us how we too can invest our lives for eternity, even as the ones whose stories are told here have done.

—*J. Christy Wilson, Jr.*
Emeritus Professor, World Evangelization, Gordon-Conwell Seminary

Introduction

Why do we like stories? Is it simply curiosity? Or is it because a story can help us with some new information, truth or insight?

Long before our ancestors learned how to write things down, they were already sharing family traditions and helpful information through story-telling. For our ancestors, some of those stories contained information that could mean the difference between death and survival.

Through his parables, Jesus used story-telling to share deep truths and insights about God and about life with those around him. Although some of Jesus' parables were not written down until many years after he told them, they were not forgotten. These vivid stories had been valued by his hearers who found them easy to remember.

This book seeks to carry on this story-telling tradition in a meaningful way. Here mission stories about Christian people from 16 countries are presented. These stories can be used as illustrations for sermons and talks, and as stories to read to children. Older children can read them without help. The stories can also be adapted into dramas for use with church school groups, or at camps and conferences.

Please join in my prayer that these stories will help many people – and will glorify Jesus Christ, the greatest story-teller of all.

You will know the truth, and the truth will set you free (Jn 8:32).

1

Ariet's Search for Love

One day the nurse at the missionary clinic at Akobo, Sudan, was surprised to look up and find that a lovely young African girl had arrived at the door, crawling. She beamed at the nurse with a proud smile for having made it there on her own.

"What is your name?" asked the nurse. "And how far did you have to crawl to get here?"

"My name is Ariet," replied the girl, still smiling. "And I crawled about two miles to get here."

After the nurse had examined the girl, she asked missionary

Don McClure to observe her and give his diagnosis of why she couldn't walk. After his preliminary testing, Don said, "I can't be sure. But it looks like she had spinal meningitis when she was small. It left her legs too weak to support her body. With vitamins and food supplements we can improve her general health – but I am afraid she will never be strong enough to walk again."

Everyone attached to the clinic was amazed at how faithfully Ariet came every day after that, unless it rained, for treatments. They not only gave her medication but also massaged her body with oil daily. Ariet really liked that massage and the staff enjoyed seeing the glow that began to radiate from her young face.

Soon Ariet insisted on staying for the daily worship services. The longer worship services on Sunday seemed to be her greatest delight.

"Why don't I send your medications to your village so you won't have to crawl so far?" suggested Don.

"Oh no!" objected Ariet. "Then I would miss the worship services. I am glad to crawl two miles to learn about God's love for me, during the church services."

After Don visited Ariet's village he began to understand Ariet's great need for God's love and for the loving attention she got when she came to the clinic or to worship, for her family openly showed how they resented having to feed her and care for her when she could do so little in return to help with the family's chores. Without intending to be, they were cruel in the way they made her feel unloved and unwanted.

Even though Ariet had learned to endure the abuse and neglect from those in her village, she desperately longed for the attention and loving care she got at the clinic and at worship services. One Sunday, after worship, she asked Don a very difficult question: "If God loves me, why can't I walk?"

"I wish I knew the answer to that question," replied Don. "But I don't. I don't think anyone knows the answer – but I do know that God loves you and I do, too. And my wife loves you and all the people here at the clinic love you."

"I know that you and the people here love me," replied Ariet. "But how do I know that God loves me?"

"Ariet, it is God who inspires us to love you. God works through us to show you how God loves. Believe me, it is God's love that led me to come to your country in the first place. Imperfect as we are, God is proving to you how much God loves you through what God inspires us to do for you."

"Now I finally understand why you came to help us," replied Ariet. "And through the worship services I am gradually learning enough about God and Christ to want to belong to God's family, just like you do. Will you baptize me when I am ready?"

Eventually Ariet was baptized and became a joyful Christian. In spite of her weak legs and abuse at home, Ariet developed a bright, cheerful personality that was amazing to everyone who met her. When other children pushed ahead of her in line she just smiled and kept on joking and laughing with them. She thought deeply about things – and seemed determined not to let her handicap ruin her life. Finally, she seemed convinced that God did love her.

To further show his love for her, Don began carrying her the two miles home on his shoulders. Villagers began to ask each other, "Why does he do that? Maybe these Christians do love handicapped people more than we do. We need to think about ways to treat Ariet better."

In talking with Lyda, his wife, Don said, "Ariet is making a great Christian witness here."

"Yes," Lyda responded, "In her own courageous way, Ariet is teaching us a lot about love and Christian dedication."

To make crawling easier, Don made special knee-pads for Ariet for she was getting big calluses on her knees, like those of a camel. Lyda gave her a pair of pants which made crawling much easier than the long dress-like shirt she had used before.

Now retired in California, Lyda said, "As far as I know, Ariet is still crawling to her church in Akobo—but she may have found a better mode of travel by now. We thought of giving her a wheelchair but those rough, rocky roads would destroy a wheelchair in a few days."

If you hear someone complaining about how hard it is to get to church, tell them about Ariet and how she crawls two miles on her hands and knees for the joy of sharing in God's love—the love she finds in worship and Christian fellowship.

2

A Revolutionary Finds Peace

Twelve-year-old Abelardo Cuadra had a secret dream-plan for his life: Someday, he would become an ambassador to Europe representing his country of Nicaragua.

When Abelardo shared his aspiration with his brother Manolo, he suggested, "If you want to go into government work here, the fastest way is to join the army. When you become a military officer you will have power, for it is the military that controls things in this country." It took a few years, but when Abelardo was old enough, he joined the army and soon became an officer, a lieutenant.

His dreams suffered a setback, however, for the closer Abelardo got to the center of power in the country, the more he realized that the person controlling Nicaragua at that time was a cruel dictator named Anastasio Somoza.

Being a lover of justice and freedom, Abelardo joined a rebel group that tried to overthrow the dictator. The attempt failed and Abelardo barely managed to escape into the neighboring country of Costa Rica. His dream-plan to become an ambassador had failed. In hiding in Costa Rica Abelardo took a job on an isolated banana plantation. One day a stranger came up to him and asked, "Are you Lieutenant Cuadra?"

"Yes, I am," replied Abelardo.

"I have an interesting offer to make to you," said the stranger. "Please come with me."

Abelardo went with the stranger and was introduced to a small group of rebels who had vowed to fight for justice and freedom in Panama. "We will give you $5,000 and a position in the new government if you will join us," said the leader.

To the hot-headed Abelardo, this sounded a lot more interesting than spending his life on a steamy banana plantation, so he joined them. But this small revolution also failed so once again Abelardo fled to Costa Rica. This time he escaped by way of Cuba. In Costa Rica he settled down in the town of San José where he tried his hand at several civilian jobs, including that of a prize fight promoter. Soon he met and fell in love with a lovely, brown-eyed Costa Rican girl named Aida.

Aida was attending services at a Protestant Christian church and, because he loved her, Abelardo agreed to attend some services with her. Abelardo liked the church services and soon, along with Aida, he became an active member.

Eventually they got married. Not long afterwards, Abelardo

heard of another attempt to overthrow the Nicaraguan dictator, Somoza. For the fiery revolutionary Abelardo, the temptation was too great. Without telling his wife about the revolution he simply said, "I am going away on a trip. I will come back as soon as my secret business is finished."

For the third time Abelardo fought in a revolution – and for the third time the revolution failed! When he escaped back to Costa Rica Aida was very angry and upset with him for doing this foolish thing. But she forgave him and accepted him back into her life.

In spite of Aida's urging that he become a man of peace, Abelardo joined a fourth revolutionary battle. This time he took the side of the Costa Rican government thinking this was the right thing to do. He promised Aida, "This is my last military fight."

It was almost his last act in life, for again his side lost and Abelardo's life was saved only because he took asylum in the Mexican embassy. No longer able to stay in Costa Rica, Abelardo took his wife and two children with him and went to make a new life for his family in Venezuela.

Aida lectured him, "You have learned that war and violence are not the best way to fight for justice and freedom. Why not try the way of education and persuasion? Why don't you become a school teacher?"

Since becoming a Christian, Abelardo had learned a lot from Jesus Christ, the Prince of Peace. He had to agree with Aida and realized he could do more for the cause of justice and freedom by teaching than by the use of guns and bullets, so he took a job teaching in a public school in Venezuela.

All would go well until he started talking too much about justice and freedom in his classrooms; then his supervisor would move him to another school. Finally Abelardo thought,

"Maybe the Protestant mission schools will allow me a little more freedom to talk about justice and democracy."

He went to see a missionary in Caracas, Dr. Alan Hamilton, to ask for a teaching job. "We don't have a job opening in Caracas," said Dr. Hamilton, "but we could make you the head of a small mission school in the isolated town of Guatire. Are you willing to accept that challenge?"

Agreeing to try, Abelardo found that it was indeed an ordeal. The faltering school had only twelve students. By hard work and a lot of loving, tender care for his students, Abelardo slowly expanded the school (*Colegio Americano*) to 80 students—quite a large number for such a small town. With the help of a local missionary, Rev. Harry Peters, they got some gym equipment and started a gymnastics program during the day for the school's students, but then at night they opened the gym up to young people of the entire town.

This program became very popular and Aida began to use the gymnastics program as an evangelistic outreach, giving Christian tracts to all who would accept them. Abelardo and Aida had their membership in a church in the nearby town of Guarenas but since there was no church in Guatire, they started a Sunday school program with 25 charter members, some of whom were their own students.

Abelardo coached the town's weight-lifting team so well that they won the championship for the entire area. His students also won most of the marching contests they took part in during local district parades. Abelardo won such acceptance in the community that he was eventually allowed to join the Venezuelan public school teachers in laying flowers at the foot of the statue of Simon Bolivar, the "Great Liberator" who helped bring independence to Venezuela, Colombia, Ecuador, Peru and Bolivia.

After the ceremony, Abelardo mentioned in a speech that the battle for justice, freedom and democracy that Bolivar worked for was not yet quite complete. This remark was reported to the government and Abelardo was arrested and put in jail. When he was able to show the police chief the actual text of his talk, Abelardo was released, for the police recognized that he was the victim of some local jealousies.

Returning home, Abelardo said to Aida, "Now I know that I am a Christian. Before, I would not have rested until I had taken revenge on my accusers. Now I not only forgive them, I don't even want to know who did it!"

One day the dictatorial head of a nearby country visited Venezuela. Since years before he had been in the same rebel training camp with Abelardo, he decided to go greet his old friend. Standing on the edge of the crowd, Abelardo watched the dictator appear decked out in his military uniform and flanked by guards armed with automatic rifles. Abelardo turned away and left. He no longer wanted to speak to this swaggering man of violence.

When Aida heard of his reaction, she said, "See how much Jesus Christ has changed you! Christ has transformed you from a man of war to a man of peace."

As the years passed, he became more eager to tell others about Christ, who could change a violent person into a peacemaker. Instead of being a diplomat for his own country he became an ambassador for Christ and often joined Rev. Harry Peters in evangelistic trips all around the area. Now at age 86, Abelardo is retired and living in Caracas. Do you agree with him and Aida that it is best to use education and persuasion to work for justice and peace? Don't you think we would have a better world if more people asked Christ to make them into peacemakers instead of resorting to war?

3

Danger in Africa

Five-year-old Margie's day started off with bad news.

A Sudanese neighbor came running up to her missionary father and said, "Yesterday a lion killed two of our Shulla people near here. A man was hoeing his field when he disturbed a sleeping lion. The lion jumped on him and tore his throat. His wife ran for help. A Shulla neighbor ran up while the lion was eating the first man. The neighbor threw his spear but missed. Then the lion mauled the neighbor so badly that he also died. By this time other men came and finally killed the lion with their spears."

Margie and her father were both glad to hear the lion was dead, for if it were still alive, Margie's father would have to hunt it down and kill it with his gun. Otherwise, no one in the village would sleep safely until the killer lion was dead. After hearing this scary news, Margie wanted to stay near her father for the rest of the day. That meant she had to go with him on a boat ride across the river to take a load of tall grass which was needed across the river to make a roof for the church.

The native-style long canoe was piled high with the grass. On top of the grass was a wheelbarrow which a young Shulla boy kept in place by sitting in it. Margie was sitting between her father's knees as he piloted the boat across the river with an outboard motor brought from America. As they chugged merrily along, suddenly the boy on the wheelbarrow yelled, "Look, there's a crocodile on the bank!"

"Bring my gun to me and I will shoot it," called back Margie's father.

As the lad started toward Margie's father with the gun, he lost his balance trying to walk across the slippery grass piled high in the canoe and fell to one side. The canoe tipped over in the swift-flowing current and everybody, and everything, in the canoe went under the water, including a second Shulla lad standing at the front of the canoe.

Margie came up sputtering and coughing, but she didn't seem to be afraid. Her father grabbed her and started swimming for the bank. This seemed like a lark to Margie, but her father became frightened when he saw the crocodile slide off the bank and into the water. The two lads quickly got to shore, but in the swirling water it was all Margie's father could do to get her safely to the bank, away from the rushing water and the threatening crocodile. When they were all safely out of the

11

water, Margie said, "Daddy, that was *fun!*"

He laughed and said, "Well, I didn't think it was fun. When I saw that crocodile slip into the water I could already feel his sharp teeth biting my tummy. I'm glad he didn't decide to have both of us for his lunch."

Margie's father and the two Shulla boys finally fished everything off the bottom of the river except one lost shovel and a missing saw. When it was dried off, even the outboard motor seemed to work fine. Fortunately the "croc" had vanished.

When Margie's mother heard about their mishap, she was horrified. "Don't you ever take Margie in an overloaded boat again!" she exclaimed. "It's too dangerous."

"Don't worry, I won't," replied Margie's father. "One awful experience like that is enough to last a lifetime."

"Yes," replied Margie's mother. "If we expect to live long enough to teach the love of Jesus Christ to these Shulla people we must learn to be more careful."

Thankfully, they did live carefully enough to complete more than 40 years of missionary service in Sudan and Ethiopia, but Margie never forgot her dangerous river experience under the watchful eyes of that crocodile. When she got older, she wondered why she thought it was so much "fun" that day.

Some activities which seem like "fun" at the time can actually be life-threatening. What about you? Have you learned that the "fun" of riding your bike too fast down a hill can be dangerous? Or that chasing each other around a swimming pool can cause someone to fall and get hurt? Do you remember that the famous Christian handicapped writer and artist, Joni Eareckson Tada, broke her neck diving into a pool that was too shallow? Do you know that "fun" with drugs can become addicting?

Let's all learn to keep our "fun" out of the danger zone.

4

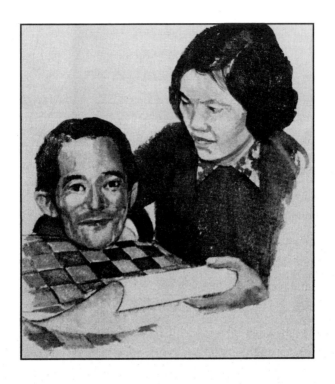

Genzo, a Poet of Japan

Nine-year-old Genzo Mizuno felt sick–very sick. His stomach was cramping painfully and his whole body was burning with fever. Seeing how ill he was, his mother, Umeji, rushed him to the hospital in their small Japanese town of Sakaki. It turned out Genzo had a severe illness from which many people were dying.

Genzo did not die from the illness, but another terrible thing happened to him. With his resistance lowered, he got a form of brain fever (like polio), which left him completely paralyzed. He couldn't move his arms or legs. He could see and hear, but he couldn't speak. The only thing he could move freely were his eyelids. He could still blink.

Since the hospital was unable to do anything more for him, Genzo's mother began taking care of him at home. It was like taking care of a newborn baby. Genzo couldn't even cry to let his mother know when he needed to be turned over in bed. He became very depressed.

After hearing of his illness and depression, a local Christian pastor came to visit Genzo. He told Genzo that all people are made in God's image. By sending Jesus Christ into the world to love and help us, God showed his love for everyone – even paralyzed people like Genzo.

Genzo blinked his eyes rapidly to show he was interested. The pastor began coming to visit Genzo often and always read the Bible to him.

When the pastor couldn't come, Genzo's mother and younger sister, Miyuki, read the Bible to him. After reading the Bible for several months, and with some special training from the pastor, all the family became Christians. There was now a new note of hope and joy in the family.

With her own hope renewed, Genzo's mother was determined to find a way to help Genzo communicate his needs, feelings and thoughts. She had an idea.

One day she came to Genzo and said, "Look at this big chart I have made. It contains the basic phonetic sounds of our language (ka, mi, so, yu, etc.). I am going to put this large chart on the wall and point to the various phonetic sounds with this long stick. When I touch a phonetic sound that forms the first sound of a word you want to use, you must blink your eyes. By your blink I will know that is the beginning of the word you want to use. Then I will do the same for the second, third and fourth phonetic sounds.

Genzo was overjoyed to find he could make words and sentences in this way. It opened up a whole new world to him.

Soon after learning how to communicate, Genzo said to his mother, "I would like to try writing some Christian poems. I think that is the best way to express the new joy and peace I feel deep inside me. Now that Christ has shown his love for me, I want to tell everyone about this new gift of joy and peace."

One of his first Christian poems was:

> *I trust God for everything.*
> *I will live in peace.*

In an interview, Genzo said, "It may take me up to 30 minutes to record one poem. But with the patient help of my mother and sister, I get them written down. In my poems I want to continue to sing about God's love for me."

And God's love wasn't just for Genzo. His mother wrote in her diary, "Genzo's faith has taught me that one can lose all the visible treasures of life and still not lose faith in God."

Genzo died a few years ago, but his poems still bring joy to us.

5

A Murderer Brings Peace

"You mean I can become a Christian – even though I killed a man in a drunken brawl?" asked the man of the Niksek tribe in Papua New Guinea.

He was in prison for his crime and was talking to a visiting missionary. "Yes," the missionary said, "if you are truly sorry for what you did – and really want God to help you become a man of peace – God will forgive you and transform you."*

"For the first time since I came here to the prison in Wewak, you have given me hope," said the tribal Niksek man.

There in prison this man became a Christian and began serious Bible study. He also was determined to take Christ's message of love and peace back to his Niksek people so when he was released from prison he asked missionary Fritz Urschitz, "Will you help me to take the good news of Jesus to my people?"

"Yes, I will," replied Fritz. "What are your people like?"

"They are a people who live with hate and fear," explained the Niksek convert. "My people build their houses on platforms 30 feet high—because they are afraid of their neighbors. They live in small hamlets of two or three families but with no real sense of community. That is why they have to build homes on the top of such high poles, to protect themselves from nearby enemies."

"How should we get started telling these people of Jesus?" asked Fritz.

"I think the first thing we should do is tell them Bible stories. And then I will tell them how Christ changed me—from a violent and hate-filled murderer to a man of love and peace," suggested the Niksek convert.

Fritz and the Niksek convert took a Missionary Aviation Fellowship plane to Ambunti. From there they traveled many miles up the April River by canoe to reach the Niksek tribe's isolated jungle area.

After hearing about the love and forgiveness of Jesus Christ, the Niksek people were fascinated with this revolutionary power. They agreed to help build an airstrip near the river which opened the way for other missionaries to come occasionally and help Fritz and the original convert.

Soon more than 80 neighbors had heard the good news of Jesus and had been baptized in the April River. Still the Christian group continued to grow. When visiting missionaries who had long heard about this violent tribe went to visit this new mission station, they were amazed to see how the developing community was learning to live in peace and harmony.

While one visiting missionary, Graeme Smith, was speaking to this new Christian congregation, a heavy rain storm poured down. Rather than run for cover, everyone crowded under one of the 30-foot-high houses so the service could continue. There they had a wonderful communion service, using the elements they had on hand. They reverently passed around sections of baked taro root, their basic food, and each baptized Christian broke off a small piece of taro and then shared this with their neighbor saying, "This is the body of Christ broken for you." The "wine" they passed to each other was water from the river served in small conical cups made from folded leaves.

When it came time for the offering, Graeme was surprised to see that the only thing they had to bring as gifts to God's temple was taro, which they piled high in a wheelbarrow near the altar. Graeme thought, "This is the first time I have ever seen a wheelbarrow used as an offering plate." After the service, the taro was loaded in two canoes and taken to a needy village down the river. Soon the whole area had heard about the way this once violent community had become peaceful folk concerned about the welfare of their whole area.

Hymn singing was new to these Niksek people, but Graeme found that what they lacked in skill they made up for in enthusiasm and in a Christian spirit that radiated the presence of their savior. Years later when he returned to visit the Niksek community Graeme reported, "Today, Niksek is a model village with a school for children, adult literacy classes, a church, a health clinic and a trade-store. And there are now hundreds of believers."

During the years some customs had changed. Graeme

noticed that in the Christian communities people no longer built their houses on high platforms and were content to build their homes near ground level. This was a concrete sign that Christ had changed the Niksek people from a life of hate and fear to a life of love and peace.

In order to support the growing community and as a self-development project the Niksek people had begun to grow vegetables. Since they had to be airlifted by plane to markets in distant cities, the shipping expenses ate up most of the profit. Recently, a new source of income was found for it was discovered that their village sits on top of a gold mine. The income from this mine will support their community for many years.

Amazingly, God used a converted murderer to help bring the peace of Christ Jesus to this Niksek tribal people.

What about you? Do you know someone who is oppressed by violence, hate and fear? If so, why not tell them about the Niksek convert, whom Christ changed from a person of hate and violence into one who radiated the love and peace of Christ.

6

Orop's Sacrifice for a Friend

"Try again, Orop," said missionary Don McClure. "You keep getting the letters of your name all mixed up."

"I just can't seem to get it right," complained nine-year-old Orop, "but I will keep trying."

Orop was writing in the sand, using his finger as a pencil. In those early days Don's mission school in Sudan had no money for pencils and paper, but they had lots of fingers and sand, so they used what they had.

After working patiently with Orop for a year Don gave up

and said to him, "I am afraid you have a learning disability which prevents you from understanding things like the other children in your class do. Would you be willing to give your place in class to a new student?"

"Yes, I will do that, but please let me listen from outside the school window," begged Orop. Even this led to a problem. Orop would try repeating the stories he heard about Jesus to little groups of children he would get together. But just like the letters of his name, he got the stories all mixed up and this confused the little children.

Don finally decided that, for some reason, Orop's brain had never fully developed. His head was not round like the others, but flat on top. Yet he could take good care of his mother's goats and could make a toy goat out of mud to play with. He was also one of the most loving and loyal of all the children.

"I must find some church job that Orop can do well," thought Don. Finally he got an idea and asked Orop, "How would you like to be the official carrier of God's Book (the Bible) when I go on evangelistic trips to the nearby villages?"

"Oh, that would be great!" exclaimed Orop, jumping up and down with joy.

From then on Orop became known as "The Official Carrier of God's Book." And he did his job well. After a few trips to the villages with Don, Orop had learned to sing several simple songs. Soon he began to run ahead of Don as they neared a village. He would have the people gathered and singing by the time Don arrived to give his message about the love of Jesus Christ.

One day Orop was with a group of small boys playing in the river. Suddenly a big crocodile grabbed one of the boys in its mouth. The rest of the boys ran away but Orop jumped into the water and began fighting the huge crocodile. With his bare hands he succeeded in making the crocodile drop the little boy, but the crocodile grabbed Orop in place of the other boy.

Hearing about it, Don ran to the river with his gun. He saw the crocodile come up for air with Orop in its mouth. Afraid he might hit Orop, Don waited for a better shot. The next time the crocodile came up it didn't have Orop in its mouth and Don shot it. But all they could find of Orop was one arm and one leg.

Don thought, "Greater love has no man (or boy) than he who gives his life for a friend" (Jn 15:13).

After the funeral, when the mangled body was lovingly buried, Don went to comfort Orop's mother. She said, "Orop told me he was not afraid to die, because Jesus would come to take him by the hand and lead him home. Is that true?"

"Yes, that is true," replied Don.

The mother said, "Will you teach me about Jesus? I want to be with Orop and Jesus."

In a letter Don wrote to his parents in America he said, "Orop never owned a pair of shoes, never learned to write his name and couldn't finish first grade, but when the roll is called up yonder—he will be there."

Let's all try to pay more attention to the people in our community who have learning disabilities. Maybe, like Orop, they can teach us a great deal about love and loyalty.

7

Rosita Braves the Altiplano

"Daddy, our Sunday school teacher said we need national missionaries to start more Protestant churches here in Argentina," said twelve-year-old Rosita Shehirlian. "Do you think I could become a national missionary when I grow up?"

"It is true we need more Protestant missionaries," replied her father. "We have lots of Roman Catholic churches but only a few Protestant ones. I had hoped you would become a secretary in my business office, but if you want to become a home missionary I don't see why not. Why don't you start praying about it and see how God may lead you."

"I will pray, Daddy, I will!" exclaimed Rosita, her brown curls dancing in the air as she nodded her head vigorously in agreement.

After graduating from a state teachers' college, Rosita did graduate work at the famous Union Seminary in her home city of Buenos Aires. Then she was given a national missions assignment in the town of Alejandra. She had two jobs to do there. One was to be the Christian education director in a small Protestant church and the other was to try to start a new church in a village nearby.

Her first step toward starting the new church was to call on homes there. One night she went to visit a friendly lady she had met earlier but when she knocked on the door she found herself in the middle of a wild drinking party. Not knowing what else to do, she said *"Buenos noches"* (Good evening) in a shaky voice.

The loud voices became quieter and the lady of the house said, *"Buenos noches, Señorita.* What can I do for you?"

"I am visiting from the Protestant church in Alejandra," answered Rosita. "But I see you are busy now. Maybe I should come back later."

One of the drunk men staggered to his feet and said, "Ah, you are one of those *evangelicos.* I have heard the preaching in the plaza." He raised his glass of red wine and said, "This is the blood of Jesus Christ, which cleans us from all sins. That's what they say—these *evangelicos.* I like that talk." Then he keeled over in front of Rosita, breaking the glass and spilling the red wine on the brown dirt floor.

At the older woman's request, Rosita came back to visit the next Thursday afternoon. The woman had her daughter-in-law with her. Both of them seemed interested when she told them about God's love and forgiveness through Jesus Christ.

This eventually led to regular Christian meetings twice a week. The two women invited their friends to join them and soon there were nine rural women in the group. Later, with help from the Protestant pastor in Alejandra, this small group became the foundation for a new congregation.

But not everyone was happy with Rosita's work. She had persuaded one of the men who had been at the wild drinking party to marry the woman he was living with. Soon their children started attending Sunday school. Some other men didn't like that. One of them said, "We must get rid of this meddling 'wall worshipper.' Those Protestants worship bare walls, without any pictures or statues of saints on them, and she is trying to make too many changes around here."

Occasionally children threw pebbles at Rosita, but there was no really serious trouble. With the help of local Protestants, she bought land in the village and built a simple church building. Most of the work was done by local Christians, with some financial help coming from Rosita's family and friends in Buenos Aires. Her father and mother were very proud of the good work she was doing.

Soon Rosita turned the successful new church over to students of Union Seminary in Buenos Aires and announced she was ready to help with another pioneer project. Rosita expected to begin a new job in Rosario, a city near Buenos Aires, but a leading pastor in the area requested she consider becoming a missionary teacher and start an experimental school for Aymara Indian girls in Bolivia.

At first Rosita refused the invitation saying, "That is too far away. I hear the Aymara girls are very poor; and the work would be too hard for me. I have taught school in Alejandra, but I have never headed up a school myself. Besides, the altiplano (high plateau) where they live is too cold in winter."

About a week later Rosita couldn't get to sleep so she started reading a book about a Protestant missionary couple in China who had been killed by enemies of Christianity. She thought, "This couple was willing to give their lives to share God's love with the Chinese people. Surely it is not too much for me to face a few hardships in the country of Bolivia."

So she agreed to try to start the experimental school for Aymara Indian girls. Soon she was off to serve them in the isolated town of Ancoraemes, Bolivia, which turned out to be a dusty, bumpy six-hour bus ride from the Bolivian capital city of La Paz. The elevation was 11,500 feet.

When Rosita stepped off the bus a cold rain was falling and her feet sank deeply into the mud. She tried to pull loose. Her foot came out, but her shoe remained stuck in the brown mud. She thought, I have just arrived and already I am bogged down!

Finally she was rescued by the waiting missionary couple who had invited her to come. Giving her a *poncho* (raincoat) to keep off the cold rain, they took her to see the building where she would live and start her experimental school. It was a former military barracks and Rosita was disappointed to find it had no electricity, no running water, no inside toilet—no modern conveniences at all. Even the doors and windows wouldn't shut properly.

"What do I do about bedding and food for the girls?" asked Rosita.

"Oh, they will bring their own bedding and food from home," answered the missionary. "You will have six to eight girls, ages ten to 15. They will go back home on weekends."

Rosita found that the girls did bring plenty of food: rice, beans, cheese and *chuno*, a blackish potato paste cooked with cheese. When Rosita tried to add eggs and milk to the diet, the girls said, "We don't know how to cook eggs. Eggs and milk are our 'cash crops.' We sell them to traders for use in the city. That way we get money to buy the sugar, coffee and clothing we need."

Teaching the girls to read and write was hard enough, but Rosita found it even more difficult to teach them new habits. Since it was cold at that high altitude the girls wore several skirts and seldom took baths. In fact, there was not a single bathtub in the whole town. Finally, Rosita taught them to use washbasins and to launder their outside skirt once a week and their inside skirts twice a week. They also learned to use pesticides, to keep the lice out of their hair.

Rosita came to love those girls as they did her. One girl wanted to become like Rosita so much, she did something forbidden by her family and cut off one of her long, black braids so she would have short hair like Rosita's brown curls. Happily, Rosita persuaded her to leave the other braid on her head so she would not be kicked out of her family.

Once Rosita served the girls cocoa, thinking it would be a tasty treat. But the girls spat it out saying, "You have burned the coffee!" Rosita drank it alone.

The experimental school became a success, thanks to the love, patience and hard work of Rosita and those who supported her. Today the school has more than 30 students and has moved to a fine new building. Many of the girls have become Christians and are now sharing God's love with their family and friends.

With God's help, Rosita did a lot more good work than she ever dreamed. What interesting things do you think God could help you do with your life?

8

Francis, a Kenyan Evangelist

Francis, an African boy, spent his childhood years in the big city of Nairobi, Kenya. He was very smart and ambitious. When anyone asked him what he wanted to be when he grew up he always answered, "I want to be president, like President Jomo Kenyatta." Francis was proud of his newly independent nation of Kenya and of their first African president.

But Francis' strong will sometimes led him to disobey his parents. One day, when he was five, his mother was cooking a large pot of soup to feed her large family. "Mama, I'm hungry. Can I have some of that soup right now?" asked Francis.

"No, we will all be eating soon, so just wait a little while," said his mother.

But Francis disobeyed his mother and tried to get the hot soup by himself. As a result he pulled the whole pot of boiling soup down on himself burning his arms and legs so badly he had to spend many months in the hospital. Just when it looked like the doctors would have to amputate his legs they got better, in a miraculous way. Francis' mother saw this as an answer to her prayers that God would help to save her little boy's legs.

Francis' father was a wealthy businessman who owned several shops and stores. Francis' older brother, who managed the business, got a bad case of malarial fever which settled in his brain and caused him to make some bad decisions. His mental confusion led to the loss of most of their shops and money. All that was left was enough to buy some land out in a distant country village where the family moved and opened up a small shop for food and household items. Francis was nine when this happened and felt very sad to leave all his friends and live a much poorer life than before.

In the new village, the long, dry season made it seem like a desert. Water had to be bought from a rich man's well five miles away. One day Francis' mother said, "Francis, I want you to go with your brother to the well and bring back as much water as our donkey can carry."

"It's too far away, Mama," answered Francis. "I know I can ride the donkey to the well, but I will have to walk five miles back when the donkey is loaded with water jars. I don't want to go and I won't!" said the rebellious Francis.

To get away from his mother, Francis ran across the room toward the door. Along the way he bumped the stove and knocked off a kettle of boiling water. This time the water scalded his upper body, especially his head, face and shoulders. He was in the hospital for three months. Finally he healed with no bad scars to show for the burns his disobedience had caused.

Although he sometimes disobeyed his mother, Francis really loved and respected her for the way she taught her children the Bible and took them to church regularly. Seeing how her faith helped her in rough times, Francis began to want to become a Christian himself. After attending church for many years Francis was invited to go to a youth camp when he was 14 where he made his decision to become a Christian.

Francis not only had a godly mother but he also had an older Christian friend, Peterson, who had been expelled from his home for becoming a Christian. Peterson had suffered but with God's help had taken care of himself since the age of twelve. Francis admired his faith and determination.

When Francis was 17 he entered the East Africa School of Theology and began studying Bible and evangelism. Two years later he became a student minister and began preaching in nearby churches and outdoor evangelistic meetings in local marketplaces. The school leaders recognized his gift for evangelism and appointed him to start new churches in the area.

Francis agreed and began to start a new church by his evangelistic preaching. Then as soon as he got together a small group of new Christians, he would ask another young pastor to take over. At this point Francis would move on to start another church in a new location. Usually the churches began in someone's home. As the group grew they would build a small chapel with mud walls and a thatched roof made from palm branches. When it grew even larger, they would build a permanent church of concrete block or other appropriate building material. This way Francis helped to start 19 new churches.

Wanting to become a better evangelist and church leader,

Francis came to America to study at Fuller Seminary in California. Recently he said, "God did not lead me to become president of my country of Kenya, but God did lead me to work for Christ's Kingdom, which is much greater than my nation of Kenya. Therefore, I feel my present job of helping to build new churches in Africa is more important than being president of Kenya. My dream is to get a doctor's degree in mission work (missiology) and go back to start many more new churches, not only in Kenya, but also in the surrounding nations as well: Uganda, Tanzania, Somalia, Sudan, Zanzibar and Ethiopia."

Francis had to make some sacrifices to come to study in America. Not only did he leave his interesting work with the 19 churches he started but also he left behind his family and friends in Kenya. He is now 28 but has delayed marriage until he can get his studies completed and again be settled in mission work in Africa. To support himself at school, Francis works at a rescue mission for homeless people called the "Door of Hope" where he helps feed, house and counsel many homeless people who live on the streets of Pasadena.

Francis' friend, Peterson, once lived on the streets of Nairobi after his parents kicked him out of their home for becoming a Christian against their wishes. Even though he was homeless for a while, Peterson worked hard and became a successful businessman and now owns his own home. Francis hopes that some of the homeless people he is helping in Pasadena will be able to do the same.

In working for the Kingdom of God, Francis is working for a Kingdom much greater than his native Kenya since God's Kingdom includes all the countries of the world. What are your plans for the future? Would you like to join Francis in working for the wonderful Kingdom of God?

9

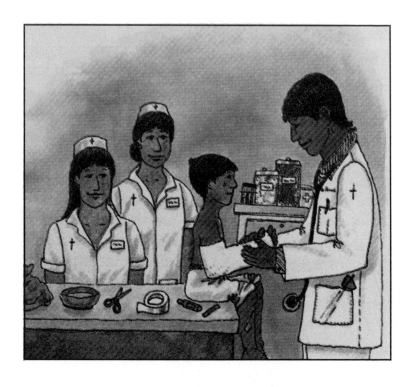

The Mayans' First Doctor

In the small Mayan town of Xocenpich (Shokenpeach), Mexico, news travels fast. One day the exciting word came, "Manuel has a new bicycle. It is the first bicycle anyone in this town has ever owned."

Nine-year-old José Estrella went to see it. The bike was painted red and had shiny silver handlebars. José couldn't help feeling a little jealous of Manuel. He thought, "Someday I will have a bike like that."

But a few days later, there was some upsetting news about

the bike: "Manuel fell off his bike and broke his arm. It's too bad we don't have a medical doctor here in Xocenpich to fix his arm so it will heal quickly."

Soon this was followed by the sad news: "Manuel is dead. His broken arm had developed a bad infection. With no trained medical doctor in the area to help him, he died in spite of all that our local witch doctors did to try to help him."

Villagers began to fear bikes. José didn't realize it at the time, but this experience was the first step that led to his becoming Mexico's first Christian Mayan doctor. José's father was one of the first Mayans in Xocenpich to learn to read and write. He did it through the aid of the famous missionary Dr. Frank Laubach, who visited the village in 1943 and helped him to learn to read and write his own Mayan language.

José's father was also one of the first Mayans in his village to become a Protestant Christian. Although a poor farmer, he decided he wanted to give his five children the best education he could obtain for them.

José's older brothers attended the small one-class village school in Xocenpich that educated them through the second grade. José was a fast learner. He could read and write before he started his two years of classes at the village school.

From age ten to thirteen, José was taken out of school to help his father plant corn and do farm work. When his older brother insisted that José join him in getting more education in mission schools away from home, José's father finally agreed. With the help of missionary scholarships, José finished grammar school and high school in the Protestant Mission School in Merida.

A missionary, the Rev. Ted Finley, started the now-famous Southeastern Bible Institute in Xocenpich in 1942. He befriended José. Young José decided to dedicate his life to Christian service as a doctor.

With the encouragement and help of Ted Finley and another missionary, the Rev. Fred Passler, José graduated from the School of Medicine of the University of Mexico in 1956. He then completed his medical internship. Although he could have made more money by becoming a doctor in one of Mexico's big cities, José decided to go back to his childhood village of Xocenpich which had now grown to about 500 people but still it had no doctor.

With the help of some Christians in Oakland, California, the Christians were able to start a small clinic-hospital in Xocenpich. Based at the clinic, Dr. José began to serve the medical needs of his Mayan people in Xocenpich and the surrounding villages. He was assisted by two Mayan nurses trained at a missionary hospital in Morelia. Later the clinic added a school to train nurses' aides. After their training, these nurses' aides would start their own small clinics in other villages.

When Dr. José first started his work at the clinic, the local Mayan people were a little wary of him. They couldn't decide whether to go to this new Christian doctor or to the local witch doctors they had been using for many years. But José gained everyone's respect when he saved the life of a twelve-year-old boy. From then on, Dr. José Estrella had more patients than he could ever have hoped for.

The work at the clinic-hospital in Xocenpich was enough to keep him busy, but José couldn't rest. He knew that thousands of Mayans in the surrounding areas had no medical care. He eventually bought a small truck and started traveling to nearby villages.

One of the missionaries who helped in the Mayan work, Fred Passler, was the pilot of a mission plane. With Fred providing plane services, José was able to extend his medical services to villages hundreds of miles away.

Dr. José still continues to serve the needs of his Mayan people in Xocenpich. Sometimes, when he is out in the surrounding villages, Dr. José does double duty as a preacher leading evening worship services.

And now that there is a doctor in Xocenpich, the people's fear of riding bicycles has been overcome. Within three years after Dr. José came to serve in Xocenpich, there were more than 20 bikes in the small town!

With a smile, Dr. José says, "Now we have enough bikes for a good bike race here in Xocenpich. If people get hurt, I will be glad to take care of them."

10

From Sudanese Slave to Minister

"Run and hide! The slave-traders are coming!" shouted baby Toobia's father. "Take the baby and hide in the swamp!"

Toobia's mother snatched up the one-month-old baby and ran as fast as she could, with her husband right behind her. They hid in the tall grass but the slave-traders followed them and tried to find them. Taking advantage of the trees and covering in the swamp, Toobia's father escaped, but his mother was captured when baby Toobia started crying and revealed their hiding place.

Heartbroken that his wife and baby son had been captured, Toobia's father sneaked into the Arab slave-trader's camp that night and tried to rescue them. As he was untying the ropes around his wife's legs, a slave-trader saw him and captured Toobia's father also.

This happened in south Sudan, but the slave traders took them to the city in the north, Khartoum, to sell them. There Toobia's mother and father were separated and sold to different slave owners. His father died in a few months, but his mother was determined to stay alive as long as possible to take care of Toobia. Yet, under the cruel treatment of the life as a slave, she died when Toobia was only six.

Toobia's slave owner said, "Toobia, your mother and father are dead now and, at age six, you are too small to do enough work to make it worth the food I must feed you. I will give you your freedom – if you will go live on the streets of Khartoum and take care of yourself."

Young Toobia was lonely and scared, but he knew he had no choice. He made his living by begging, taking left-over food from restaurants and doing whatever odd jobs he could find to make a little money. Being smart and energetic, he found enough work to keep himself healthy in mind, body and spirit.

When he was about 30 years old he learned about a mission school in Khartoum and became eager to study there. He came to the school and said, "I will work for the school in any way you want me to, if you will just teach me to read and write." And so he was accepted on a trial basis.

It was strange to see this tall, black man sitting in classes with young boys eight or nine years old, but he didn't mind. At first the boys laughed at him, but when he began to get better grades than they did, they stopped laughing – and soon came to love and respect him.

After Toobia finished his primary school studies he wanted to go on to a secondary school, but there was no secondary mission school in Khartoum. Discovering that he could enter a secondary mission school in Egypt, Toobia decided to go there, but since he had little money, he walked most of the 1,200 miles from Khartoum to Assiut, Egypt. To avoid being robbed, and possibly killed, by the roving bands of Arab bandits along the way Toobia traveled at night – when it was also cooler to walk across the burning sand. It took several months to get there but he plugged steadily on.

One night, as he was nearing Assiut, he heard moaning sounds coming from the side of the road. He investigated and found a wounded and naked Arab traveler who had been robbed and badly beaten. "Water! Give me water!" called out the man in a faint voice.

Remembering that it was Arab people like this man who had sold his mother and father into slavery, Toobia was tempted to leave the man lying there. But Toobia had become a Christian while at the mission school and it changed his way of thinking. Remembering Jesus' story of the Good Samaritan – who stopped to help a wounded man by the side of the road – he also remembered Jesus said, "Love your enemies. Pray for those who persecute you" (Mt 5:43-44). So Toobia gave the wounded man a drink from his own canteen. Using his undershirt as a bandage, he stopped the bleeding from a long gash on the man's head. Then he fed the man with some of the bread and cheese he had in his knapsack. Finally, leaning on Toobia for help, the injured man was able to limp on beside Toobia to a nearby village where help was available for him.

After graduating from the American Mission Preparatory School in Assiut, Toobia went on to graduate from college. He was still eager to learn more, so he enrolled in the seminary in

Cairo and prepared to enter the ministry.

When he graduated from seminary, one of his teachers said, "We could make good use of your talents working in the church here in Egypt. What are your plans?"

"I think I should return to Khartoum and help the church there—right in the midst of the Arabs who sold my mother and father into slavery," answered Toobia. And that is what he did. He became a very popular and successful pastor serving a church in Khartoum.

Even though slavery is now officially outlawed in Sudan, it still continues. Some African tribes still raid one another. They not only steal cattle from one another but also steal wives and children. Some tribes think nothing of killing the husbands so the wives and children can be taken as their slaves.

Let's all pray that God will raise up more fine Christian leaders, like Toobia, to help end slavery in Africa, and everywhere.

11

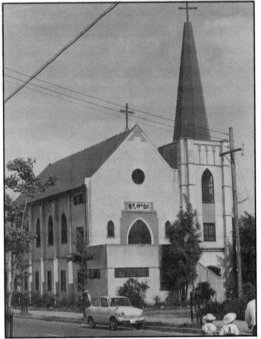

Kawachi Nagano Church begun by Pastor Yoshino

Takeo Becomes a Christian

It was twelve-year-old Takeo's turn to bat on the playground of his school in Nara Prefecture, Japan. He swung hard and heard the sweet crack of the bat against the baseball, but to his horror the ball flew far off to the left and crashed through the schoolhouse window.

As everyone watched in shocked silence, a teacher came running out of the schoolhouse. "Takeo, you bad boy," he shouted, "Can't you ever learn to do anything right? Now, look what you have done!" Red in the face, the teacher ran up to Takeo and slapped him hard on the cheek.

"I didn't mean to do that, Teacher. It was an accident," said Takeo. Without thinking what he was doing, Takeo did a very bad thing and slapped the teacher's face! Now everyone was in shock, especially Takeo. He knew his quick temper had gotten him into big trouble. He wanted to say he was sorry but he was so frightened he couldn't say a word. In Japan teachers must be respected almost like gods.

"You will pay dearly for this, Takeo Yoshino," yelled the teacher angrily. "You just wait until I tell the principal. He will expel you from school forever!"

Thinking they might also be punished, Takeo's friends laid down their baseball gloves and shied away from him. No one would even speak to him any more.

When they heard about it, Takeo's parents were also frightened and ashamed. What would become of their son? Was his life ruined forever? How could they explain their son's terrible behavior to their friends and neighbors?

Takeo and his parents were called in to see the school principal the very next day. "Your son has done a very evil thing, Mr. Yoshino," said the principal. "Students are not allowed to talk back to their teachers in this school, much less slap them. Your son could be sent to reform school for what he did. How do you think he should be punished?"

"I apologize for my son's behavior, sir," said Takeo's father. "His hot temper made him lose control and do this bad thing. Now he is very sorry for what he has done and wants to make it up to that teacher and to the school in any way he can. Please give him a second chance. He makes good grades in school and wants to become a good student in every way. I guarantee he will behave in the future."

After they had talked for a long time the principal said, "Because you are a highly respected man and a leader in our community, I will give your son a second chance. I have decided that his punishment will be as follows: He will be suspended from school for one month. He must do odd jobs to earn enough money to pay for a new window. During his month of suspension you must teach him at home so he won't get too far behind in his studies. After returning to school he must stay after school every day for a month and clean the blackboards and erasers."

"Thank you, sir," said Takeo's father. "I am sure my son has learned his lesson and will be good from now on."

As they were leaving the principal said, "Now, remember, if Takeo misbehaves like that again he will be expelled."

Knowing the importance of education, Takeo struggled to control his hot temper and stay out of trouble. He also studied hard and made good grades and finally graduated from high school with honors and passed his college entrance exams on the very first try. His good friend, Nobuo, failed the entrance exams and had to attend a special college preparatory school for a year before trying again. Hearing this, Takeo was glad he had studied hard.

One day, early in Takeo's second year in college, he received a letter from his mother saying, "Your friend Nobuo has failed his entrance exams for college a second time. It was such a great blow to him that he became very despondent. Last Tuesday he went into the mountains near his home and took his own life."

Hearing this about his good friend, Takeo became very sad and depressed. His college roommate, who was a Christian, noticed Takeo's gloom and said, "What is the matter, Takeo? You look so sad!"

Takeo told his roommate about Nobuo and then asked, "Why do you think he would do a tragic thing like that? I know college education is important, especially in Japan where you need it to get a good job, but I can't imagine anyone being so upset about failing entrance exams he would want to take his own life!"

"Well," said his roommate, "as a Christian I have come to believe that without knowing the love of God we are all in danger at such times of despair. We need God's love to give us confidence and hope that we can overcome our problems. Was your friend a Christian?"

"No, and as you know, neither am I," replied Takeo.

"I hope you will become a Christian, Takeo," said his roommate. "Then you will come to understand that God loves you just as you are, even when you fail. I failed my first entrance exams to college. It was then that my pastor convinced me that God, and my Christian friends, still loved me. That gave me the confidence and hope I needed to try again, and I passed on the second try."

Takeo thought about all these things for a long time. Finally he made two decisions. One was to become a Christian, like his roommate; the other decision was to become a school teacher so he could help despondent students like his lost friend before it was too late.

After Takeo completed his college education he took a teaching job in a junior high school in a small town south of Osaka. He liked his job teaching math; however he soon noticed that his students had many problems. Some were fooling around with alcohol and drugs and almost every day some student complained to him that a wallet or purse had been stolen, probably by another student.

One day after school as he was boarding the train to go

home, someone ran up behind him and jerked his briefcase from under his arm. Like most Japanese Takeo carried his money there. Turning quickly to see who it was he found himself face to face with one of his own students. "Taro! What are you doing?" he exclaimed in a shocked voice.

"Teacher! I didn't know it was you!" replied Taro. "If I had known, I wouldn't have done it. Here, you can have it."

Taking his briefcase back Takeo said, "I could report this to the principal, but he might expel you from school for doing this. Come to my home tomorrow night so we can talk about it and decide what to do."

The next day Taro came to Takeo's home and said, "Teacher, I apologize for trying to steal your briefcase. Please give me a second chance."

"First, tell me why you did it," replied Takeo. "You have been behaving well, and making good grades at school. Why would you risk everything by doing a foolish thing?"

"Well, I am not sure what made me do it," replied Taro. "But the main reason is that I want a bicycle and my parents are too poor to buy me one. I could save them a lot of money in bus and train fare if I had my own bike."

"Do you want a bike bad enough to work for it?" asked Takeo. "If you will come and work in my vegetable garden after school and on holidays you could soon earn enough money to buy a bike. Do you want to try that?"

With a big smile on his face Taro said, "That would be great, Teacher. When could I start?"

"Tomorrow, if you want to," replied Takeo. "But there is one more thing I would like you to do. You need to learn about God's love for you, so you won't do bad things any more. I am planning to start an evening Bible class in my home on Saturday nights for students who have problems and may want to come. Would you want to come?"

"Yes, I would," replied Taro. "I know I need to become a better person."

Takeo started the Bible class and gradually more and more students joined it. Taro was one of the first ones to make his decision to become a Christian. One of the students who came regularly to the Bible class was a boy named Saburo who failed his entrance exams into high school and came to Takeo for counseling. "I failed in both math and English," said Saburo. "Could you help me with those two subjects so I can pass the exams next time?"

Remembering how his friend Nobuo had taken his life, Takeo replied. "Of course I will help you. But I can help you with math only. I don't know English well enough to be much help. However, I have an American missionary friend living nearby who can help you."

After receiving tutoring from Takeo and the missionary Saburo did pass his exams. He became another person from the Bible study group who became a Christian.

One day Takeo found a note on his desk from the principal, "Come to my office after school. I need to talk to you."

Wondering what it was about, Takeo went to the office. When he got there the principal said, "Is it true that you are inviting students to your home for a Bible class? And is it true that some of them have become Christians?"

"Yes, that is true," replied Takeo, wondering why the principal would ask such questions.

"This is a school, not a church or temple," the principal replied sternly. "I must ask you to stop using your influence as a teacher to make Christian converts."

"But I only do it in my own home. I never teach Christianity in my school classes," replied Takeo. "Surely that is not against Japanese law."

"No. It is not against Japanese law, and I can't stop you," said the principal, "but it is against the Japanese spirit of Shinto and Buddhism. Joining a foreign religion like Christianity might make young people disloyal to the emperor in time of national crisis. I do not have the power to stop your Bible classes but I have the power to fire you from your teaching job if I think it is in the best interest of the school and of our country."

Takeo was disappointed and upset. He had not believed the principal would be so narrow minded. Finally he decided to resign his teaching job and enter seminary to become a Christian minister. He thought, "It is not enough to teach my students school subjects. I must teach them about God's love and forgiveness. They need God's help and the presence of Jesus Christ to help them overcome their problems."

After Takeo finished seminary he came back as he had planned and founded the first Christian church in that small Japanese town where he had started his Bible class.

Do you face any problems which you need God's help in overcoming? If so, why not let God help you as he helped Takeo?

12

Zia, a Blind Afghan Christian

As he was enrolling in the NOOR Institute for the Blind in Kabul, Afghanistan, 14-year-old Zia Nodrat thought, "I hope they can teach me to read books using the Braille system. Then I can learn a lot more about this mysterious world around me — which I cannot see."

Zia was an unusually intelligent boy. He had already memorized the whole Koran, the holy book of Islam. That would be like one of us learning the whole New Testament in Greek, for the Koran is written in Arabic, which is not Zia's native language. Zia amazed his teachers at the Institute for the Blind by completing the six primary grades of the Institute in three years.

Not only did he finish his schooling in half the time it took most students, but while studying in Braille he also learned English by listening to, and repeating, the English he heard on a transistor radio. Soon he began listening to Christian radio broadcasts, such as "The Voice of the Gospel" coming from Addis Ababa in Ethiopia. One day he said to a friend, "After listening to Christian broadcasts for a long time I have decided to become a Christian. I have accepted Jesus Christ as my personal Savior."

"Do you realize that in Afghanistan you could be killed for becoming a Christian?" asked his friend. "Don't you know the Islamic Law of Apostasy (law against leaving Islam) says you can be killed for changing your faith?"

Zia answered, "Yes, I have counted the cost and am willing

to die for Christ since he has already died on the cross for me."

Later, Zia became the spiritual leader of the few Afghan Christians he knew. Although most of the students in the Institute were Muslims they elected Zia president of their student association. But the next year, after it became known that he was a Christian, he lost his second try for student president. One of Zia's Christian teachers said, "I am sorry you lost the election, just because it is unpopular to be a Christian."

"That's all right," replied Zia. "As John the Baptist said, 'I must decrease so Christ can increase' " (Jn 3:30).

Seeing his son's zeal, Zia's father said, "Before he entered the Institute for the Blind Zia was like a cold and unlit piece of charcoal. Now he is like a brightly burning, red-hot coal."

Zia became the first blind student to attend the regular schools in Kabul for students who could see. He used a small tape recorder to record everything his teachers said. Then he would listen to it until he knew it thoroughly. Out of several hundred students he became the top one at his grade level. Afghan schools held special exams for students who wanted to take them. Studying hard during his three-month vacation periods, Zia took these special exams and thereby completed two grades each year.

After high school Zia decided he wanted to study Islamic Law so he could defend Christians who might be persecuted for their faith. He entered the University of Kabul and graduated with a degree in Islamic Law. At the same time he studied Calvin's famous *Institutes of the Christian Religion* and became well acquainted with this great Reformation leader's teachings.

As if that was not enough, Zia also attended the Goethe Institute in Kabul to learn German. He then began reading the many German books in Braille given to the Kabul Institute for the Blind by the German Christoffel Blind Mission.

As a top student at the Goethe Institute, Zia won a scholarship to go to Germany but when the Germans learned he was blind, they withdrew his scholarship – fearing he couldn't be independent. Zia wrote back, "What would I have to do to meet the requirements in German?"

A letter came back saying, "You would have to travel alone and take complete care of yourself without special help."

Zia answered, "I can do that. Let me come." He not only did go, but he became the top student in advanced German there – in competition with prize-winning students from other Goethe Institutes around the world. Having become a "genius" in language study, Zia translated the New Testament from Iranian Persian into his own Afghan Dari dialect. This was published by both the Pakistan Bible Society in Lahore and the Cambridge University Press in England.

Finding that too many of the Institute for the Blind students were becoming Christians, the fanatic Muslim leaders in Kabul closed the institute. When the Communists took over the country soon after that, they reopened the institute – with Zia in charge. However, when Zia refused to join the Communist party he was forced to resign.

Zia was put in prison and used his time there to learn another language – Russian. While in prison the Communists gave Zia electric shock treatments in an effort to "brainwash" him into becoming a Communist. It didn't work. Zia kept his Christian faith and was finally freed.

Knowing that millions of Afghan people had become refugees in Pakistan because of the civil war, Zia felt that God was calling him to be a missionary to the Afghan people in Pakistan's refugee camps, but he knew the Communist leaders would never approve his going there. So Zia worked out a plan. With the help of a blind beggar friend he dressed in beggar's rags and the two of them started walking toward Pakistan. It took them twelve days to walk the 150 miles to Pakistan, going over the dangerous Khyber Pass. At every checkpoint along the way Zia let his blind beggar friend do the talking and they got safely through.

Learning the difficult Urdu language of Pakistan, Zia preached in local churches – along with his work with refugees. He also began translating the Old Testament into his Dari language. In addition, he completed a book of Bible stories for children in his Dari dialect. On March 23, 1988, Zia was kidnapped by a fanatical Muslim group called "Hisbe Islami." Because he knew English, he was accused of being a CIA agent for America. Because he knew Russian, he was accused of being a KGB spy. Because he was a Christian, he was labeled an "apostate from Islam" and he was threatened with death.

He was beaten for hours in an effort to make him confess to being a spy. He would not do so because he was not a spy. It was soon reported that this fanatic group had murdered him. When the same group captured two Pakistani Christians for carrying relief supplies to the refugees, the captors said, "Don't worry, we are not going to kill you the way we killed Zia Nodrat." After being tortured, the two Pakistani Christians were released.

Some people would say we should remember Zia because he was an intellectual genius. But don't you think we should remember him for more than that? Isn't he a martyr – a Christian martyr who sacrificed his life to bring the good news of Jesus Christ to his Afghan people?

Today, Zia's wife and two of his four children have been granted refugee status in the United States. Christian friends here are trying to show their love and respect for Zia by taking care of his widowed wife and fatherless children.

13

Village of Life

Years ago, when missionaries Don and Lyda McClure first settled in a village of the Anuak people in Ethiopia, they heard some interesting comments. Not realizing that Don and Lyda, who were light-skinned, knew their language, the Anuak people, who were dark-skinned, talked among themselves as they watched them building their new missionary home.

Seeing Don's red hair and reddish, sunburned skin, one Anuak man said, "Wouldn't it be too bad to be born red like those people?"

The Anuaks, who ate only one meal a day, couldn't understand why these strange mission workers had to eat three times a day. One Anuak woman said, "They are like animals, for they eat three or four times a day!"

First Don and Lyda lived in a tent with mosquito netting. The people could see through the tent. One Anuak woman said, "I wouldn't want to live in a house like theirs. We can see everything they do."

Another thing that amazed the Anuak was the amount of furniture the McClures had. One man said, "Look at all the things they have. Already they have brought three truckloads."

Most puzzling of all to the Anuak people was why these new people had come to live in their village. A woman asked a friend, "Why do you think they have come to live in this country?"

Her friend answered, "They will probably die soon because they are not used to our heat and mosquitoes."

Don wrote to his parents, "Our battery-operated radio brings happiness to the village people. They think the music comes out of the little box and that somewhere inside, a man is hiding and speaking."

Even more amazing to the Anuaks was the "little box that speaks Anuak." That was the tape recorder that Don and Lyda used to record the Anuaks' conversation. The tape recorder was a source of joy and wonder in the village.

In the years that followed, these Anuak people grew to love and respect Don and Lyda as they got to know them better. In times of famine, Don and Lyda shared their food with these new friends. Many Anuak lives were saved through the clinic they started. Because of the loving work of Don and Lyda, the Anuak people decided to rename their village to honor these missionaries. The original name of the village had been "Acada" but after the missionary clinic helped so many people, the Anuaks renamed it "Pokwo," meaning "Village of Life."

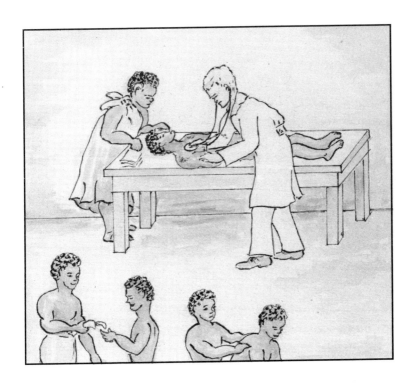

14

Missionary Clinic at Pokwo

"Help! Help!" screamed ten-year-old Arit. Her Anuak father ran out to the water ditch where she was playing and saw that a large crocodile had her by the left leg, shaking her in his huge jaws.

Since the ditch had only about two feet of water in it, her father was able to jump on the back of the crocodile and yell for others to come help him. Soon enough people arrived to hold the crocodile until they could kill it with spears and clubs.

When they brought Arit to his clinic in Pokwo, Ethiopia,

Missionary Don McClure saw the crocodile had broken the bone of her left leg, tearing much of the flesh away. Her right foot was also smashed by the crocodile's jaws. With prompt medical care to stop the bleeding and penicillin to prevent infection Don was able to save Arit's life. She would always walk with a limp, but she did not die from bleeding and infection—as many children had before Don started his clinic.

Sometimes little babies were brought into the clinic with their bodies covered with putrefying sores. Don reported, "There is no greater joy to a missionary than to see these little children begin to heal and their flesh become clear and clean as we treat them with penicillin."

Even though Don had no official medical training, because the people there lived so far from the closest doctor, he finally set up a small, simple clinic where he could dispense common medications. The most typical diseases treated at the clinic were tropical ulcers, sore eyes and malaria—which Don found fairly easy to treat and cure. More difficult were the severe wounds from spears and clubs—received during village fights or in encounters with wild animals.

Saddest of all, because they were so unnecessary, were the wounds of those who received deep cuts and burns from witch doctors who in their misguided belief inflicted these cuts to "drive out the evil spirit" that "caused" the sickness.

Don had to handle the clinic work in addition to many other duties, so he normally opened the clinic from six to seven every morning. On Sundays Don would open the clinic much longer, treat many more patients and then lead them all in a service of worship. One month Don reported, "This past month I treated 1,408 patients, even though I had to be away seven days. Always there are more women and children than men. The poor sick babies are the worst."

One time there was an epidemic of whooping cough in the neighborhood and Don had to treat from 15 to 25 babies every morning. But he was happy to do it for, without his care, many of those babies would have died from the complications of even a seemingly simply disease like whooping cough.

The most difficult case Don had to treat was a young man who had been badly beaten by the brothers of a girl he had mistreated. Don wrote, "They didn't kill the man but he would have been more comfortable (perhaps) if they had. They beat him with clubs from head to foot and left him a mass of pulp and bruised flesh. He will survive–but with fewer teeth and many scars." After Don did what he could to make the patient comfortable, he sent him on to a distant hospital for he had no way to deal with severe cases brought to his clinic.

Every morning Don would find 40 to 60 people outside the tent of his clinic, waiting for medicine and treatment. Soon they began to have evangelistic services for them every morning and teach them songs and Bible verses along with medical treatment because they realized that their spiritual needs were as great as their physical ones.

More and more patients appeared at the door and Don reported to the mission board, "It is sometimes difficult to get all the medical supplies we need. We have torn up all our old bed sheets for bandages and Lyda has started to rip up my shirts and nightshirts for bandages."

Don and Lyda were giving the shirts off their backs to help the villagers in Pokwo, Ethiopia, who needed medical attention, just as they were giving their lives for these people who needed their spiritual ministrations.

15

A Group Wedding at Doleib Hill

"Elder La, what do you think of the idea of remarrying your wife in a Christian wedding ceremony?" asked missionary Don McClure. "Would it help in your efforts to make your home a Christian home?"

After thinking a moment, Elder La answered, "Yes, I think so. As you know we Shulla people have the custom of buying our wives just like we buy a cow or sheep. The pagan ceremony is like sealing a business contract. A Christian ceremony would show people we value our wife as a gift from God."

When Don asked La's wife about it she said, "If my husband agrees to do it I will be happy to have a Christian wedding. La doesn't beat me like most Shulla husbands do, but this would show others that he doesn't intend to marry other wives, even though he can afford to buy one or two more."

When Don talked it over with his wife Lyda, she said, "Wouldn't it be wonderful to hear her say, 'I take you, La, to be my *Christian* husband.' Most Shulla wives never take anything but beatings, curses and hard work. A Christian wedding would show she and La really love and respect each other."

After it was explained to the other elders in the church, five more elders and their spouses agreed to join La and his wife in a group Christian wedding. Some of these wives had been bought over 20 years before, but for everyone this big step toward forming Christian homes was an exciting joint project. Don worked out a wedding ceremony in the Shulla language based on the ceremony he and Lyda had used when they married. The vows to "love and honor each other until death do us part" was the central theme, but a few things were changed since they did not plan to exchange rings as this would be an unnecessary problem for the Shullas.

The wedding costumes were based on Shulla customs and consisted of a simple white cloth tied across the shoulder and draped over the body in the Shulla fashion. It seemed a little strange to have children from ages three to fifteen taking part in their parents' wedding, but their presence indicated the whole family's intention to become *Christian*.

Some non-Christian Shullas laughed at these couples but for the Christians this was a happy, proud celebration of their love for God and one another. They knew they were starting a wonderful new tradition for Shulla people. On the afternoon of the group wedding the church was filled with curious people. Everyone wanted to see how it would work out. After the ceremony all six families were invited to Don and Lyda's home for a joyful wedding feast. Delicious meat and rice were the main dishes. Everyone sat on the floor and each family had a common dish which they shared with one another.

Don reported, "It was the first time some of the husbands and wives had ever eaten a meal together. Usually the wife prepares the food and then the husband eats. What is left the wife eats alone. If there are children the husband eats first, then the children and last of all the wife. The wife does not dare place her hand in the dish with her husband and thus make herself 'equal' with him."

"But," continued Don, "as the first step toward Christian equality we urged them to eat together at the wedding feast. At first some of them seemed reluctant to break this Shulla custom—but they soon entered into the Christian spirit of it and we had a grand time. It was harder for me, though, since I tried to be polite in the Shulla way and honor all six couples by eating with them in turn—I nearly burst!"

In the months and years that followed, Don and Lyda rejoiced when they noticed their Shulla Christian neighbors not only eating together as a family, but bowing their heads in prayer before the meal. These Shulla Christians had started a new custom for their Shulla people. Thankfully, all of the six original Christian wedding couples succeeded in setting good examples for other Shulla people around them. Today, the Christian wives of the Shulla people have become equals with their husbands—in a Christian home dedicated to love for God and one another.

Missionaries help bring many new, loving customs into the life of needy people in isolated places. Don't you think these missionaries deserve to have our prayers and support?

16

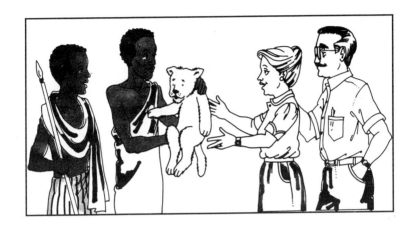

The Missionary Lion

One of the most interesting things that happened to Lyda and Don McClure during 47 years of missionary service in Sudan and Ethiopia involved a young lion cub who was later called "the missionary lion." After a big grass fire, some Sudanese hunters found a baby lion that had become separated from its mother. The cub was too small and weak to survive on its own. They took the baby lion to Lyda and said, "Would you like to have this lion cub as a pet for your baby boy, Donnie?"

Knowing that the cub would certainly die if someone didn't take care of it, Lyda said, "Thank you. I am sure our son would enjoy having that cub as a pet." They named the little cub Sheba. In the following months, the baby lion and baby boy became good friends and played together.

When time came for the McClures to return for a visit to North America, Lyda and Don had to make a decision. Should they take the lion cub with them or should they leave it in

Sudan? "Let's take Sheba with us," Lyda said. "She can help us as we speak at youth conferences." Don agreed. Little Donnie was happy to hear that his new pet was going with them.

On their way home, the lion was the main topic of conversation with people all along the way. When boarding the ship at Alexandria, Egypt, Don bought a ticket for each of them—including one for the pet lion. The ship agent said, "I'm sorry, but a lion is not on the list of things allowed on this ship."

"Please let me see your list," Don asked. The agent showed it to him. Don noticed there was a category called "jungle cat." "This lion is a jungle cat," said Don. Finally the agent allowed them to come on board.

As the months passed, the lion began to outgrow Donnie since baby lions grow much faster than baby boys. The young lion had a habit of standing on its hind legs with its front paws on Donnie's shoulders. He was just like a big, friendly dog. This was all right when Sheba was small, but now she was a half-grown lion. Her weight began to knock over little two-year-old Donnie. Lyda said, "I think we are not going to be able to keep Sheba much longer. She has grown so big that she knocks Donnie over. After all, Sheba is a wild animal. She can't be expected to be gentle with Donnie forever."

"You're right," Don agreed. "Let's see if we can find someone to provide a good home for her." Finally they found a famous lion trainer who would be glad to have her.

When they delivered Sheba to the trainer, they explained how they had rescued her from the wild and how they had used her for mission conferences. "Well," said the trainer, "I have seen lions do many things, but this is the first time I have seen one do mission work."

Isn't it nice to know that sometimes one of God's wild creatures can serve as a "missionary"?

17

Lyda, the Healer

Lyda and her husband, Don McClure, came to world attention when he was killed by Somali guerrillas in Ethiopia in 1977. Much has been published about his life and work, but Lyda, who shared his missionary adventures in Africa for 47 years, has always remained in the background. But her life has many lessons for all of us.

When Lyda first graduated from college she took a teaching job for three years in a girl's school in Khartoum North, Sudan. There this slim, brown-eyed girl with curly brown hair met Don McClure, whom she found to be "red-headed, rash and religious." These two short-term missionaries eventually married and returned to Sudan as a missionary team.

Even though Lyda put a lot of energy into caring for her home and raising children, she always had time for evangelism, teaching and reaching out to help her neighbors with their problems. She soon found that many African women who became her new friends would follow her advice on nutrition and child care.

When the McClures were moved to the isolated new mission station at Akobo, the British provincial governor advised Lyda, "The only way the government will allow your family to stay in that out-of-the-way place is for your family to keep in good health. If any become sick you will have to leave – and not return. Remember, this is malaria and black water fever country. Protecting your family will keep you busy."

Though far away, Lyda found life in Africa was quite exciting. Her first night at Doleib Hill she heard wild animal noises nearby. Don got his flashlight and rifle to go out and investigate. She heard a shot and soon Don returned saying, "It was only a jackal."

The next morning they found a huge python draped over the limb of a nearby tree. He had swallowed the mate of the jackal whole, so that was why the jackal had been howling. Soon their neighbors from the Shulla tribe came and skinned the python, removed the jackal whole and then skinned and ate it, too. That poor jackal was eaten twice: once by the python and then by the Shullas.

Since the McClures depended on antelope they hunted for their meat supply, Lyda became Don's hunting partner. They found the best time to hunt was at night and Lyda carried the light while Don carried the gun. Usually they hunted gazelle, water buck, a small antelope called *orbi* and a larger one called *tiang*. In time, although Lyda was only five feet three inches high, she became as good a shot as Don and proved her proficiency with a gun by shooting down flying ducks and geese, using a small, but powerful, 22 "Hornet" rifle.

Lyda found herself handling much of the work at the medical clinic, where she was basically self-taught by reading medical books given to her by a doctor who had to leave the field. Soon she was quite proficient at caring not only for minor ailments but also for teaching good nutrition and child care to her neighbors who came to depend on her advice.

In addition to caring for her own children at home, teaching them with the famous "Calvert System," Lyda saved the lives of many orphaned or abandoned babies put in her care. It became apparent that Lyda had a special healing touch and she was able to bring babies who had malaria, severe diarrhea, whooping cough and various fevers back to health. The love she radiated in caring for the babies brought many people to Christianity because many of these babies' relatives wanted to know what made people love as she did.

The McClures had been sent to their isolated mission station during the depression years so their supporting churches couldn't send them much help. With no funds for a new missionary home, Lyda and Don decided to build four native huts, side by side, connected by screened-in passageways to make the house mosquito-proof since this was malaria-mosquito country. The walls and floors were made of mud and each hut had a conical grass roof.

One advantage to living in these huts was that the local women felt comfortable visiting Lyda there and easily became friends with her. One of Lyda's best friends was a local woman named Om Omot (meaning "mother of oldest son, Omot").

The first day Lyda moved into her new mud-walled house Om Omot came to visit and showed Lyda how to keep the mud floors smooth by putting on a top covering of wet sand and smoothing it by hand. This flooring was fine for the local people's style of living, but Lyda found the legs of their Western-style beds, tables and chairs dug holes in it and she was constantly having to wet the sand and smooth it by hand. Thankfully, Om Omot seemed to often appear at the right time to help her.

One day Om Omot said, "Your two children, Margie and Donnie, seem to be so healthy. Most of us lose about three out of five children before they grow up. Please teach me what you have learned about proper feeding and health care for children." Thus Lyda began to share her experiences, including how to kill the bacteria in cow's milk by boiling it and how to keep her pots and pans clean. Also since the local diet of millet, meat and fish was short on vitamin C, Lyda encouraged her new friends to eat limes, grapefruit and papayas. Thankfully, Om Omot went on to have five children without losing a single one.

Seeing the loving way Lyda cared for her own family, took in needy babies and helped others, Don's good friend, Gila, said to him, "I want to have a house just like yours."

"That should be easy," replied Don, "You helped to build this one."

"Oh no," Gila explained, "I mean I want a *home* like yours, where the wife knows that 'God is love,' and where the family relationships are based on love."

Lyda's loving actions were drawing many people to the faith just as Jesus said, "By this shall everyone know that you are my disciples—that you love one another." But it wasn't only her loving care that made Lyda famous; it was also her fearless attitude towards the difficulties that appeared – whether that meant driving their old International pickup truck across a dangerous swamp or throwing a shoe at a rat. It was famine time and rats, as big as squirrels, were eating up all the local grain. One night Lyda looked up and saw a row of big rats sitting on a ledge just outside their home. Taking her shoe she flung it at the rats with all her strength. The aim was right on and one huge rat fell dead at her feet. The next morning she won the eternal gratitude of a neighbor by giving him the rat for the first feast of meat he had enjoyed in weeks.

As a young girl Lyda was very shy, afraid to speak in public. In her college speech class she would often lose her voice when it came her turn. But, after a few years in Ethiopia, Lyda had overcome so many strange difficulties that she no longer feared crowds and so became a very effective speaker – whenever she had to for various church groups. In helping to heal others, she had been healed herself.

18

Missionary to Quezaltenango

Paul Burgess had been named after Paul in the Bible because his parents hoped he would grow up to become a missionary like the Apostle Paul. His minister father, who had died of T.B. when Paul was eight, had been too sick to do overseas missionary work. He hoped that Paul could carry out his dreams.

When Paul was in college he applied for a job as "Sunday school missionary" with the American Sunday School Union. God blessed his efforts for in one summer he started eight new

Sunday schools, a prayer meeting and a preaching point. To do this he traveled 1,130 miles by foot, bicycle and wagon during that summer.

He liked that work so much he thought, "Maybe my parents were right. Maybe God is preparing me to be a missionary to another country."

He studied so hard in college that his roommate said, "Why don't you take time to go out on dates with girls, like the rest of us do?"

"Well, if I am to go on to seminary to become a missionary I must get good grades," answered Paul. "Besides, my high school girl friend may still be waiting for me, even though she never answered my last letter. And I am too shy to ask her why."

"Are you still angry with her because she got the top honors in your high school, making you come in second best?" asked his friend. "Or are you just too cowardly to write her?"

These questions led Paul to write his girlfriend, Dora McLaughlin, asking why she never answered his last letter. This time she answered and seemed willing to continue their friendship.

Paul graduated from seminary, married Dora and was appointed as a missionary to Guatemala. But there was a problem. Like his father, Paul got sick with T.B. He won a scholarship to study in Germany and France, but had to come home after one year in Germany because of his T.B. After a long period of medical treatment and rest, he recovered enough so he and Dora could sail to Guatemala in 1913 on the United Fruit Company ship *Saramacca*.

Because of his good grades and graduate study, the mission board had assigned Paul to head up the mission schools in Guatemala but when he got to Guatemala the local mission leaders changed his assignment to evangelistic work in the Quezaltenango province. He was disappointed because he was looking forward to working in the schools, but he said to Dora, "If God is calling me to evangelize Quezaltenango, I'll give it everything I've got!"

At first the work was difficult. At the time, Latin American Protestants were not popular. People threw stones at Paul as he preached. Once, in the city of Sija, someone threw a stone through a window and hit Paul on the left leg. Later he learned that just for listening to his preaching one woman had been beaten and others were refused food when they tried to buy it in the Sija shops.

Slowly Paul made progress. He opened a Christian bookstore, started a monthly church magazine and baptized 64 converts in one year. Some of the converts were city leaders. Soon he had earned such respect in the area that people started calling him "Don Pablo" (Honorable Mr. Paul).

After awhile he bought a used printing press and began producing his own Christian books and pamphlets. His evangelistic work brought such good results that within four years he was supervising 25 congregations.

One of the newly converted families left Quezaltenango to work on a distant cattle ranch called "El Reposo." When Paul tried to go visit them there, the German ranch owner refused to let him hold a worship service for the workers, saying, "Our religion is work. No noise, no music or talking permitted."

Disappointed, Paul went on his way toward the nearest town. Just before he got there, a group of soldiers approached and said, "You are under arrest."

"Why?" asked Paul, completely surprised.

"The ranch owner telegraphed us. He said you are trying to stir up trouble among his workers."

The mud floor of the prison smelled bad and there were no beds for Paul and the other prisoners to use that night. A kindly drunk man invited Paul to share his blankets made out of gunnysacks. Thousands of fleas made his night miserable, but the next morning a kindly officer let Paul go.

One of Paul's congregations was made up primarily of German immigrants. When two young men from that group climbed a nearby mountain, they were killed by 30 witch doctors who accused them of camping on "sacred ground." The witch doctors threw their chopped up bodies into the volcano crater as a sacrifice to the gods of the mountain.

Paul decided that he must work with the Indians to save people from the mistaken cruelty of the witch doctors. Later Marcelino Vasquez, a wealthy leader of the Quiche Indians who was himself a witch doctor, was converted. He became a famous evangelist winning many Indians to Christ and starting a new church at El Palmar.

It took a long time to get mission board approval and support for his Quiche work, but Paul finally succeeded and began the Quiche Bible Institute with only two students. By the end of the first year there were nine Indian students studying to become evangelistic leaders and today the institute has over 100 students.

Once Paul was arrested because he had written critically of the injustices of the dictatorial government of General Ubico in his magazine *Tio Peruchos*.

While in jail Paul gave his Spanish New Testament to a friendly young guard named Antonio Muñoz. Imagine his happy surprise when, years later, he attended a church service in a distant town—and found that Antonio Muñoz was the Christian pastor of that church!

Paul was a great missionary scholar and evangelist who

started over 100 new churches, wrote 23 books and published four Christian magazines. Dora translated the entire New Testament into the Quiche Indian language, with some help from Paul.

Just a few days after Christmas in 1958, Paul died in Guatemala of a sudden heart attack. The Guatemala newspapers were filled with his praises. However, those who knew Paul thought he would have liked best what his sister-in-law, Vera said, "No road was too steep for Paul if only he could tell just one more Indian about the Savior."

19

A Hostage in Beirut

Jerry Levin was on his way to work as head of the CNN
news office in Beirut, Lebanon. With his dark hair and mustache, his Jewish face blended in well with the other Semitic
people walking the same street.

Suddenly someone walked up behind him, tapped him on
the shoulder and said in a heavy accent, "Excuse me." When
Jerry turned around, the man pushed a small handgun into his
stomach and snarled, "You come!" Suddenly a small car
stopped at the curb and the man pushed Jerry inside, forcing
his head down on the seat.

"Close eyes! Close eyes! If you see, I kill!" he threatened as
the car sped away. They took Jerry to a nearby room where
for four hours he lay blindfolded on a bed as his captors cruelly

tried to force him admit he was a spy.

"I am a TV journalist; I'm not a spy!"

"No, you are a CIA spy!"

"I am not a CIA spy!"

"Then, you're an Israeli spy," another captor claimed.

In desperation Jerry yelled, "Why are you holding me? Where is my wife?"

"Your wife has found a new man," said one and they all laughed.

"Stand up!" shouted one of the captors. They led Jerry outside the room and made him kneel. He wondered if they were going to kill him now. Then . . .

"Lie down!" ordered one man. Putting a gag in Jerry's mouth they bound him from head to foot with brown wrapping tape. Jerry felt his circulation slowly being cut off. Then he was carried and shoved into what seemed like a truck bed. The truck roared off to an unknown destination.

Jerry calculated that if the trip took over two hours, he would probably be in the Bekaa Valley under the control of some Iranian-backed terrorists—a group called "Hizballah" (Islamic Party of God). If it should take longer they might be taking him to Iran.

They stopped in about two hours so Jerry deduced he was in the Bekaa Valley. Over the next weeks Jerry was moved from one house to another. He was forced to wear a blindfold whenever guards were present, and wherever he was kept, any windows in the room were either painted over or blocked with shutters. For over two months Jerry did not see another face or a tree or even the sun.

To keep from going crazy and try to "escape" his reality for even a few seconds, he repeated over and over lists of sports teams: football, baseball, basketball and hockey—including the names and positions of his favorite team, the Detroit Tigers. He also recalled the operas and plays he had attended and repeatedly relived his courtship of his wife, Sis.

When he found he was beginning to talk to himself he wondered if this was the beginning of madness. But he thought, "I must talk to someone. I can't talk to the guards, they won't listen. I can't talk to God because I am an atheist."

Until that moment it had seemed to him the prayers of his Christian wife were foolish – but in his predicament he began to think she might be right and he be mistaken. Maybe there was some "Higher Power" that controls the world and our ultimate destiny. But then he rationalized that it would be dishonest to pray until he could truly believe. For ten days he struggled with this "journey inward," which his solitude made possible.

Continuing his "journey inward" Jerry finally made his decision to believe in God – and in Jesus Christ. Finding himself able to pray, Jerry thanked God for this opportunity for solitude and he prayed for his family. He even began to pray for his captors, following Jesus' teaching to "love your enemies and pray for those who persecute you" (Mt 5:44).

Jerry's food was insufficient to keep him healthy so he began to lose weight. Five months after his capture, Jerry came down with a weakening stomach virus which gave him stomach cramps. The guards resented his frequent knocks on the wall for them to take him to the bathroom. Once they refused to come at all and he had to "live in his own stink."

Going to the bathroom was the only time during the day when he could stand up. Otherwise the chain that bound him was so short he could only sit or lie on his soiled pallet on the floor. Once on a trip to the bathroom he was left alone for a few moments and with his fingernail he scraped a small hole in the paint covering the window and was able to see beautiful mountains outside. The second time he was able to make out a town and in the distance beyond it he recognized the snow-covered Mt. Lebanon which confirmed his suspicion that he was in the Bekaa Valley.

As his virus worsened the guards finally called in a doctor who told them to give Jerry medicine, but they delayed for a week. The second time the doctor came to examine him he made the guards promise to give him his medicine. He also said to Jerry, "We have nothing against you as a person. But we do hate America for using the battleship *New Jersey* to lob shells into our Muslim villages – killing men, women and children."

He was still suffering from his stomach virus when Jerry was forced to read a statement written for him which was videotaped and said, "My life and freedom depend on the life and freedom of the prisoners in Kuwait." These prisoners had made a terrorist attack on the U.S. Embassy there.

Suddenly in November, after eight months of cruel treatment, Jerry's captors began to treat him a bit better. Although still not enough for a normal maintenance diet, they began to give him one hot meal almost every day. Whereas he had been suffering from the freezing cold with no heat and not enough warm clothing, the guards gave him two more T-shirts, a second pair of socks and even heavy underwear. Jerry layered on all of these and crawled under the extra blankets provided, but he was still cold. A few times they even brought in a heater for a short period.

Jerry later learned that his improved treatment was probably due to his wife's urgent appeals to the Syrian government which has great influence in the Bekaa Valley.

At Christmas in 1984 Jerry's guard announced, "We want to give you a Christmas present. What do you want?"

Jerry blurted out, "A Bible!"

Two nights later they gave him a red, pocket-sized New Testament. "Joyous Noel," said his guard.

On February 13, 1985, Jerry was surprised to find that after his daily trip to the bathroom the guard had fastened his chain very carelessly. He knew he could get free and began to plan carefully. At midnight he raised his window quietly and discovered that it opened on a second-story balcony.

Quickly he tied his blankets into a "rope" – thankful for his time as a Boy Scout. Fastening his blanket-rope to the balcony's iron railing, he let himself down onto the stony ground where there were many sharp thorns. His shoes had long since been taken away, so he was forced to flee with bleeding feet down the mountain, dodging lights and barking dogs.

After about two hours he saw lights and heard voices coming toward him. Fearing capture, Jerry flung himself under a nearby parked truck. The strangers fired shots and ordered him to come out.

"Help me!" Jerry pled as Syrian soldiers grabbed him. In spite of the shots, they proved to be friendly. His ordeal was over. Later Jerry wondered whether the guard was careless on purpose. Did his wife's pleas to Syria have anything to do with his escape? Did Sis' even-handed appeals for "honorable alternatives" to the violence being used to try to solve problems help bring about his freedom? He soon was convinced his escape was no accident and that his wife's efforts had helped him reach freedom.

Although his year of captivity was a tragic experience that Jerry hopes never to endure again, out of it came something positive. God used those hours of forced solitude to help Jerry complete an important "journey inward" – to a new life in Christ. "In all things God works for the good of those who love him, who have been called according to his purpose" (Rm 8:28).

Today Jerry works for World Vision. He is a peacemaker among Arabs, Jews and Christians and is seeking to help solve world problems through the "honorable alternatives" of dialogue and negotiation—not the hopeless way of violence and revenge. From Jesus he has learned the way of love and forgiveness.

20

Katie's African Escapades

One night Katie Turner was standing in the doorway of her missionary home in Kenya talking to a friend. She was wearing thongs so the tops of her feet were bare. Suddenly she looked down to see a cobra slither across her foot and quickly disappear into her living room—where it couldn't be found.

A little while later she found a large cobra in her kitchen so she called Jim, another missionary teacher at her school, to come and help her. Holding the snake's head with a forked stick, Jim killed it with a *panga* (a long-bladed knife). Knowing these "spitting cobras" could blind her if their poisonous venom was spit into her eyes, Katie was careful not to get too close to the snake.

This was only one of many escapades Katie had during the 32 years she served as a missionary teacher in Sudan and Kenya. Since Kenya is blessed with many wild animal parks, Katie often used her vacation time to go see the fascinating lions, zebras, elephants and other animals there. Once at the famous "Treetops" park she was bending over to tie her shoe when, for some reason, a baboon jumped across her back.

On an outing with friends at the "Hippo Pool" in Nairobi Game Park, she lost part of her breakfast to some thieving monkeys. Her friends had the car trunk open—with a large bunch of bananas inside. Suddenly several monkeys appeared, snatched the bananas and backed off to eat them. Munching happily on the bananas, they occasionally looked over at these naïve people as if to say, "Thanks for so kindly providing this delicious treat."

Even though Kenya has conscientious and able leaders, it is a poor country and many people have a hard time getting enough to eat. Knowing that education is one of the keys to gaining a better life for her Kenyan friends, Katie was glad to be a teacher at the church-related schools of Tumutumu and Garba Tula where she taught typewriting and other commercial subjects, as well as Bible classes.

When Katie first arrived to teach typewriting, there was not a single good typewriter available on which her students could practice. So she wrote letters appealing to church friends in America, who sent her 21 typewriters. She was happy with this gift, but still she had over 40 students in each class so this meant only half had typewriters to use at any one time.

Katie continued making urgent requests to her church friends in the U.S. One day she came into her classroom and found 82 typewriters taking up so much space there was no room for the students. She laughed because from being a typewriting teacher with no typewriters, she now was a teacher with too many typewriters and no students – a problem which didn't take long to fix!

Many of Katie's typewriting students won prizes but Katie was especially proud of one young man named Stephen Mwenda who not only won prizes, but went on to continue his education beyond high school.

When Stephen started teaching third year secondary school students he wrote to Katie saying: "It's certainly different being a teacher instead of a student, Miss Turner. I understand now what you went through with us. I'm trying to follow your example of firmness with understanding and encouragement."

In 1983 Katie's missionary career almost came to an unhappy end. With a family of African friends, she was on her way to enjoy a brief vacation trip to the Tsavo West Game Park. Suddenly driving on very bad roads near the park, their car hit a big pothole in the road and rolled completely over twice, coming to rest in a ditch below the road.

No one was killed in that wreck, but there were serious injuries including Katie's hands and arms, which were badly cut with flying glass. She and the family praised God that everyone survived with only painful cuts and injuries when they could have all been easily killed.

Now retired and living in California, Katie has fewer escapades than when she was teaching in Africa. She still keeps in contact through letters with many of her African "sons and daughters" and her walls are covered with pictures of African friends so she won't forget to write them. On her tables she has displayed fascinating carvings of some of the wild animals of Africa—to remind her of all the escapades she had while teaching school on that continent.

You may never serve God in an exotic land like Kenya or Sudan, but you can serve where you are. And, like Katie, your service will surely bring many enriching friendships, exciting adventures and happy memories.

21

A Gang Leader Turns to Christ

Tom Skinner, once the feared leader of the Harlem Lords gang in New York who had stuck his knife into 22 boys in gang fights, one day heard something on the radio that changed his life. At the time Tom was a black nationalist who hated the old white system which he felt kept African-Americans in poverty. He craved power to fight back at the whites for all the wrongs he and his community had suffered.

Suddenly Tom's favorite music program was interrupted by a Christian speaker who said, "All our sin, anger and spiritual suffering is caused by our separation from God. We will never be happy until we become 'new creatures in Christ' " (2 Co 5:15). Tom did want to be happy – and he knew his power as a gang leader was satisfying no deep hunger in his heart and soul. In that moment he was hooked. After much thought and prayer, Tom said to his gang, "I have committed my life to Jesus Christ, and I can no longer responsibly lead this gang."

Later, the No. 2 leader in the gang said, "When you told us you were going to follow Christ, I intended to stick my knife in your back as you walked out. But something, or someone, kept me glued to my seat. I couldn't move."

Tom told his gang buddy what Christ was doing in his life and that young man, too, became a Christian. Within a year, seven other members of Tom's old gang had joined them as new Christians and together they began to study the Bible and meet for Christian fellowship.

From that small beginning, Tom Skinner has gone on to become the leader of one of the most effective inner-city Christian ministries in the world. His outreach to urban young people tries to develop five skills they need to get ahead: spiritual and moral qualities; basic abilities in reading, writing and math; learning to cope in society and make right decisions; developing earning power (which Tom calls "bread-on-the-table skills") and leadership talents.

At his "high-tech learning center" in Newark, New Jersey, he has proved that these skills can be taught. In recent Scholastic Aptitude Test results, his students – from the city ghetto, where 95 percent of them live below the poverty level – scored 1070, which is 150 points higher than the national average.

The principal of the 2,000-student high school across the street from Tom's learning center heard that the students who entered the center were the most improved students in the school, so he went to Tom and said, "Could we send you five classes a day to do the same with other needy kids?"

The center's computers, video and audio systems speed up their learning, and all learn at their own pace. Tom says, "We deal with three groups of people. The first are students between grades 3 and 12 who come to us between three and nine in the evening. The second group are dropouts from ages 16 to 25. Then there are adults who can't read or write. All of them are developing basic learning tools."

Asked where they recruit their students, Tom says, "We deliberately choose most of our kids from homes below the poverty level. We also require that they bring a parent or guardian with them the first time they come—and we honestly tell them that we are going to teach them God's Word. In addition, we require that they bring a library card. We teach them to use libraries, computers and electronic databases."

Tom continued, "In this center we have 375 kids with seven full-time staff and about 20 volunteers helping them. Some 80 percent of our summer interns are our own graduates. All of our funding comes from churches and individuals. We do not accept government funding because it would thwart our teaching the Christian values these kids urgently need."

Through God's love, Tom is helping to overcome poverty, drugs, hopelessness and despair in the very neighborhoods which he terrorized as a young gang member. Regarding his personal faith and motivation, Tom quotes the verse, "Christ has made us one out of every kindred, tribe, tongue and nation. Christ has made us priests and a kingdom to serve our God. With Christ we shall reign on the earth" (Rv 5:9-10).

Tom adds, "Jesus is now living his life through my redeemed blackness. ... To be one in the body of Christ does not require that I have to become white."

Tom plans to put his projects in 20 cities. Tom Skinner is certainly a living example of how Christians, by working together regardless of skin color, can become effective servants in ministry. The transforming power of God's love can bring salvation to our inner cities. Thank God for the glimmer of hope Tom Skinner has already put there!

22

A Home for the Homeless

Little Peggy was tired and hungry. She was also scared—not knowing where her family could find a place to stay overnight in this strange new town of Pasadena, California.

It was almost supper time and they still hadn't found a spot. The car stopped and she heard her father say, "Wait here with your mother, Peggy, while I see if this church will give us some money for food and a motel room. We can't give up now, after having come all the way from Detroit to find work here."

Soon her father came back and said, "The pastor gave me directions to a social service center called Union Station. Maybe they can help us. We will have to hurry and get there before all the beds are taken by other people who have no money and no place to stay."

When her father went into the office at Union Station, seven-year-old Peggy went with him. "What can I do for you?" asked a young lady at the desk. Peggy liked her pretty face and sweet smile.

"We came here looking for work," answered her father. "But with expenses along the way for food, a place to stay and unexpected car repairs, we have run out of money. Could you take us in for a few days while I look for work?"

"Yes, we can provide food and housing for about a week or so," replied the lady with a smile. "If you don't find work by then, we can refer you to another place that can give you some help. We can only give short-term emergency aid."

With Union Station sponsoring him, Peggy's father did find work. He was a good mechanic and found a garage that needed someone to help with car repair work.

Union Station Foundation first got started in 1973. It was first located on Union Street. After moving three times, it is now located on 412 South Raymond Avenue in Pasadena. In the beginning, seven downtown churches participated in getting the work started. Now over 50 congregations help out, including Protestant, Catholic and Jewish groups.

Union Station can provide enough food for up to 225 people a day and it can manage housing for 56. This includes men, women and children – and those of all ages, from senior citizens to infants.

Dedicated doctors and nurses voluntarily provide preventative health care and emergency medical-care services on a weekly basis. A team of mental health care people from Pacific Clinics visits daily to dispense medication, counseling and needed referrals for the homeless, and sometimes mentally ill, people who come there. A program was also started to help people recover from alcohol or drug addiction.

Another group called Case Management Services provides assistance to as many as possible of those who come to Union Station in getting jobs, finding housing and obtaining legal, medical and financial help.

Professional artists volunteer their time to provide a weekly art program allowing people to find self-expression in art – or use art as a therapy to help overcome their problems.

To show their appreciation for such assistance and to learn to help others, those who come to Union Station pick up litter within 500 feet of Union Station twice a day. They also aid local churches in recycling newspapers, aluminum cans and glass. Once a month, Union Station sponsors a car wash so those who are staying there can earn a little money of their own.

Union Station provides many services, but the greatest thing it provides is friendship and love – to people who desperately need it.

23

Alice Goes to Japan

"Mom, do you think I could be a missionary like the lady who spoke at our church last Sunday?" asked eleven-year-old Alice Grube. "I know I can't be a minister like Dad because our church does not have women ministers yet, but we do have female missionaries!"

"Yes," answered her mother. "I am sure you could become a missionary, if you still want to after you grow up. Our church has women missionary teachers, nurses and even a few women doctors. Someday, I am sure, we will have women ministers."

In the following years, Alice met many missionaries, both men and women. Some she met at her church and others at

Macalester College in St. Paul, Minnesota, where she went to study. By graduation time she was sure she wanted to be a missionary to Japan.

Alice wrote the foreign mission board requesting that they accept her as a missionary candidate for Japan. Their answer was, "We are interested in your becoming a missionary to Japan but we have just used up our budget for Japan in the assignment of Miss Lindsey Hail. Maybe the budget will improve by next year."

Alice was disappointed, but she did not give up her dream of becoming a missionary to Japan. She prayed the budget would improve soon so she could realize her goal.

A few weeks later another letter came from the Mission Board saying, "For personal reasons, Miss Lindsey Hail has decided not to go to Japan. Would you be interested in taking her place as a teacher at the Wilmina Mission School in Osaka? We could send you to that school (now Osaka Jo Gakuin) for a three-year assignment."

Alice was overjoyed. Her prayers had been answered sooner than she expected and she arrived in Osaka, Japan in 1932, at the age of 23. From the harbor where her ship landed she took a train to Osaka which whizzed her by many fascinating sights along the way: oxen pulling plows through flooded rice fields; farmers working in the rain in straw raincoats; beautiful mountains on one side of the train and blue ocean on the other side.

During her taxi ride through Osaka to the school she saw colorful shops with tables in front of them piled high with yellow bananas, red apples and endless kinds of green vegetables. Shop owners were clattering around in wooden clogs (*geta*) and women in beautiful kimonos were buying food for their families.

When she arrived at the missionary home on the school

campus she was welcomed and politely asked to take her shoes off as she entered the house. For dinner there was big bowl of rice with a combination of chicken, eggs and vegetables piled on top of it.

"What is this dish called?" asked Alice.

"Oh, this is called *oyako domburi*," answered Grace Hereford, a teacher who had been there since 1925. "It means 'parent-child' dish. The 'parent' is the chicken and the 'child' is the egg." Alice found it to be delicious.

That night she prayed, "Thank you, Lord, for bringing me to this wonderful land of Japan. I really do feel like 'Alice in Wonderland.' Help me to do a good job of serving you and your people here."

Alice loved teaching English and Bible to her girl students and she quickly made many new friends. When the three-year teaching assignment was up, the Mission Board felt she was doing such a good job, they appointed her as a career missionary (for lifetime service).

What Alice liked best about her work was the making of new friends. Many of her students became lifelong friends, but when Japan's war with America started with the bombing of Pearl Harbor on December 7, 1941, Alice found that not all Japanese people were her friends.

The local police arrested her the day the war began and accused her of being a spy. Her examiner said, "We heard you are asking your students such questions as, 'What is the longest river in Japan' and 'What is the highest mountain in Japan?' Some of our military people believe that means you are trying to find out our military secrets."

"Oh no!" answered Alice. "To be a good missionary teacher I have to teach my students the superlative form of words like 'long' and 'high.' That only means I am trying to do my job as missionary teacher."

"I believe that you have been doing the right thing," said the examiner, "but we are at war with America and we will have to put you in the Detention Center here."

Hearing him say she was "right," Alice resolved to continue her teaching once this horrible war was over. After five months imprisonment she was given a choice of "house arrest" at her home or being sent back to America. It was a blessing that she chose to return to America for her house was later destroyed by bombing and she might have been killed.

During the rest of World War II Alice served Japanese-American people held in internment camps in Arizona, Massachusetts and Colorado. Having been interned herself in Japan, she was able to sympathize with, and help, those interned here. She returned to Japan in 1947.

During her 37 years of missionary service in Japan, Alice had over 6,000 students. For several years she taught at the coed school of Seikyo Gakuen in Kawachinagano City which she liked very much. In 1948, soon after the war, she went with one of her students for a visit to his remote mountain village. After riding many miles over bumpy roads and walking an additional three more miles to get there, her student said, "You are the first American who has ever been in our village." Alice could believe it.

Alice demonstrated her love for her students and the Japanese people in many ways. She became a tireless fund-raiser for the Reconstruction Fund which helped restore the bombed-out buildings of her Osaka Girls' School. She also developed a close friendship with a graduate of her school named Masuyo Harada who continued coming back to the school for alumnae activities. Alice and Masuyo found they were "kindred spirits" and their strong friendship continued even after Alice returned to the USA for retirement.

In praise of Alice, Masuyo wrote to a mutual friend, Mrs. Mildred Gray, saying, "What a good friend and a fine leader Alice was to all of us who knew her. ... She did everything for the glory of God."

Another special friend was the Rev. Sakao Funamoto, who for many years was the president of the board of directors of Osaka Girls' School. Since Alice lost her father when she was still a young girl, Pastor Funamoto became like a second father to her.

After Alice retired to Los Gatos, California, (her home state) in 1974, Pastor Funamoto made a special effort to come visit her in 1977. During his visit Pastor Funamoto invited Alice back to Japan, all expenses paid, for a special anniversary of the Junior College program of the school. Sadly, Alice never made it. She died of a massive heart attack just six months before she was to realize this dream of sharing in the school celebration.

Alice Grube's faithful service was recognized by two Japanese awards given her. One, a national award, is called the "Fifth Order of the Sacred Crown" and the other was a citation from the mayor of Osaka City stating, "You have contributed so much to help promote Osaka's education and culture. It is hereby attested to with deep, heartfelt, gratitude."

Alice served God and God's people, in Japan and in America, for 42 years. Do you think God wants you to serve in your country or, like Alice, in another country?

24

A Grandma's Memories

One day the pastor of a Japanese-American church said, "Grandma Toshiyuki, I would like to write down your life story. It is an important part of the history of our Japanese people and our church. What are your earliest memories?"

"Well, Pastor," answered Grandma, "as a child I remember helping my father, Kyugoro Abe, grow lettuce and pick strawberries on the farms where he worked. He wanted a son but had four daughters instead. We girls felt so sorry for him we worked harder than a son would have. He even named me

'June' which, in Japanese, sounds like a boy's name."

"Did your dad have his own farm or did he work for others?" asked the pastor.

"Being born in Japan, my father was not allowed to own land in those days. He didn't have money enough to buy land anyway, but he was treated kindly on the California farms where he worked – the Thompson farm where he grew lettuce and the Yamamoto farm where he grew strawberries. I played with the Thompson children like they were my own family." She smiled, "Some people called my father 'Shorty' but he made a joke of it saying, 'It's because I'm cute. That's why they call me Shorty.' "

"Did you go to school with *hakujin* (Caucasian) children, Grandma?"

"Yes, at the school in Blanco I was the only Japanese student. That didn't bother me, but I did want to do things the way they did. When I saw them bringing a lunch with sandwiches that looked like the spread was made of mustard, I asked my mom to make me a mustard sandwich. She was a little puzzled but she made it. Of course I couldn't eat it. Maybe it was peanut butter the other kids had. I still laugh when I think about that mustard sandwich!"

"Was your family really poor, Grandma?"

"I guess we were. But most Japanese people who worked on farms didn't have much more than we did, so we didn't think we were particularly poor. I do remember, though, that sometimes we had to paper our walls with newspapers – until we could save up enough money to buy good wall paper."

"Did you continue to work on the farm in high school days?" asked the pastor.

"No. For a while I worked as a cashier in a restaurant in Los Angeles. My salary was a dollar a day. But then, trolley car fare was only five cents and pork chops cost 18 cents a pound. I could eat a lot of pork chops at that price."

"Did your parents arrange your marriage to your husband, Michio?"

"No, Pastor. Some of my friends had arranged marriages, but Michio proposed to me. We actually went together for about a year before we got married. We then settled down to work in his father's drug store in Fresno.

"Since he was the oldest son of his family, I was expected to live with his family and take care of his mother who had heart trouble. I took care of her for 19 years."

"Was that really hard, Grandma?"

"Yes, it was. But we were Christians. Whenever I wanted to break down and cry, I pushed back the tears and prayed instead. Prayer to God is what kept me going. I also had to take care of two adopted boys, along with my own two daughters. The boys were relatives whose mother had been killed in a car wreck."

"Did you have to go to the relocation camps, as other Japanese had to do during World War II?"

"Oh yes, we all had to go. The military people gathered us all together at the Fresno Assembly Center. There I almost died from acute appendicitis. There was no hospital in the Assembly Center. The thing that saved my life was that a good Caucasian friend, Dr. Randall, took me to the Community Hospital and removed my infected appendix. Later we were sent to a relocation camp in Jerome, Arkansas."

"Was life in the relocation camp hard, Grandma?"

"Yes, it was rough, but we managed. The four-day ride to Jerome, sitting up on a slow-moving train wore me out. It almost killed my sick step-mother until we figured out a way for her to lie down. At the camp we had one living room and one bedroom with only one dining room and one bathroom for everyone in our area. We pasted pictures of flowers over the knotholes in the walls, so people next door couldn't see into our rooms."

"Were your children still small then?"

"Yes, my oldest daughter was seven and my youngest daughter was a baby, only seven months old. At the camp the baby got splinters in her hands and knees from crawling on the rough floor. We finally got some cheap linoleum for the living room which helped. In the bedroom the grass kept growing up through the big cracks in the floor all the time we were there. It was funny having to 'mow' an indoors 'lawn.'"

"Did you hate the government for putting your family in the camps?"

"I wouldn't use the word 'hate' but I did feel like a disowned child. My father was born in Japan, but I was born in America and thought I was an American. I felt the president and the country's leaders really let us down. I was so upset that, for a while, I felt I wanted Japan to win the war. But I knew that really wouldn't happen. Now I'm happy to see that our government has admitted its mistake and is paying reparations to 'redress' the wrongs done to us."

"What did you do when you got out of the camp?"

"Unlike most people we had about $1,000 in savings left here in a bank in Fresno. Using that and some traveler's checks we had, we started up our drug store again. We had to move three times but now we are back in the same building we started with before the war. My husband should retire, but he continues his work as a pharmacist, working closely with a Chinese doctor." Grandma laughed, "Since my daughter Barbara married a Chinese man we have gotten very friendly with the Chinese."

She added with a twinkle, "In fact, we took in a needy Mexican boy, Gene Lujuano, for three years, so we have also gotten quite friendly with the Mexican people." In a more serious tone Grandma continued, "All people are created by God so we should be friends, don't you think?"

"Oh yes," responded the pastor. "Remember when you were chosen 'Mother of the Year' in our county, that lovely supporting letter that Gene Lujuano wrote?"

"I certainly do. And even though his family has broken up and never been very supportive of him, he has done quite well. When he graduated from high school he surprised us by secretly asking the school principal to use our family name along with his own—so when he was called up to receive his diploma, the principal called him forward as 'Gene Lujuano *Toshiyuki*.' What a nice way that was to show our family his appreciation for making him an unofficial member."

"You have really had a hard life, haven't you Grandma."

"Yes, but it has also been enjoyable and meaningful. I wouldn't wish any of my tribulations on anyone, but I do think they may have made me a better person. As the Bible says, 'God disciplines those he loves.' " She added with a big smile on her face, "So he must love me very much!"

25

Crystal Albright and her three children

Crystal Pioneers in California

Crystal Albright was excited. This was her first train ride. She was looking forward to a new life and adventures in California. It was 1890 and California was still considered to be pioneer territory. The trip from Kansas took two days, but every hour or so Crystal would say, "Mama, are we almost there?" She couldn't wait to see what was at the end of that train ride.

Her mother, Josephine, trying to distract her would say, "No, but look out the train window. You may see a deer, an antelope or even a buffalo. Look! There goes a deer now."

Crystal's 14-year-old brother, Roy, was playing it cool and hid his excitement. Her ten-month-old brother, Wendell, was too young to know what was going on. But little Crystal was sure there were wonderful things waiting for her in California. Papa had told her about oranges, flowers and bright sunny weather there, even in winter.

Not many black families were traveling west on trains and this was the only occasion Crystal could later remember when discrimination against blacks worked to her advantage. She asked her mother, "Why are we the only ones in our train car when all the other cars are so crowded?"

"Well," replied her mother, "the law requires that blacks and whites ride in separate cars. Since we are the only black family on this train we get to have a whole train car to ourselves. I'm glad the custodian keeps that coal stove going. This December weather is too cold for baby Wendell."

Crystal's mother didn't mention another reason why the black porter was so kind to them but she wondered to herself whether the porter gave them special attention because she was a white woman married to a black man. Or, maybe it was because they had three cute kids.

The family was moving to California hoping to find greater freedom from discrimination. Crystal's father, George W. Albright, had grown up as a slave boy on a big plantation in Mississippi. When he married Crystal's white mother the discrimination grew worse, so they decided to move. First they tried Illinois, then Kansas—and now they were hoping to find more freedom in California. Few other blacks were adventurous enough in those days to go that far.

Crystal's father had learned to read as a boy when he worked hard to keep the wood-burning stoves fired up in a girls' school in Mississippi. The white teachers and students helped him even though it was then against the law to teach a slave to read and write. When the Civil War ended and slaves were freed, Crystal's father completed his education in Mississippi. Later he entered politics and was elected to the state senate. That's when he married Crystal's white mother—a schoolteacher from the north.

Before moving his family to California, Crystal's father had gone ahead to prepare the way. He worked out a farming partnership with a Mr. Reynolds and prepared a home for his family to move into upon arrival. Crystal was overjoyed when she saw their new house in the farming area of what is now Hollywood. "Look at the orange trees, Mama!" shouted Crystal. "Look at the tall corn—and the vegetables—and the flowers. This is like summer in Kansas—and it is almost Christmas."

The Reynolds children were Crystal's first new playmates. Soon she was also playing with Mexican children from the Lopez family and friends from the Japanese, French and German families who moved into the neighborhood.

Like many of their farming neighbors, Crystal's family were self-sufficient in almost all their needs. They even made their own Christmas presents to give one another—including homemade candy and delicious popcorn balls. They grew their own fruit and vegetables—and even the corn and other grain to make bread. They had chickens, ducks and turkeys and sold the extra eggs for money to buy coffee, tea, sugar and salt from stores in Los Angeles. Crystal's mother even made most of their clothes, buying gingham and calico for ten cents a yard.

There was a small neighborhood church where the family worshipped. Crystal's mother played the pump organ there and later played the organ and piano for other churches. She was an active Christian leader and it was her strong faith which helped her endure the early discrimination she had faced for daring to marry a black former slave. By her mother's example, Crystal also learned to love God.

Soon Crystal's family settled on their own land in a place then known as Hesperia in Victor Valley. Behind their house ran a small stream. However, before long it became polluted from the farm waste that drained into it as neighboring farmers irrigated their crops. Soon drinking water had to be hauled in by wagon. Now, 100 years later, Crystal's water-short descendants are still struggling to find enough water for their needs.

To get more land for his family, Crystal's father fulfilled the "homestead" requirements and earned rights to a lot in distant Palmdale. He had to work the land faithfully for at least three years and live on the land for at least six months of the year. After three years he finally got his deed to 160 acres, thus becoming one of the successful pioneers in California.

Once Crystal's family was making the two-day trip it required to get to the new land in far-away Palmdale. Looking at the small gap in the mountains they had to cross, Crystal said, "Mama, how can we ever get through that little hole in the mountains? I can't even see Palmdale."

"Don't worry," replied her mother. "Your father knows the way." Later, whenever Crystal faced a difficult problem in life, she would tell herself, "Don't worry, your Heavenly Father knows the way."

All through school Crystal was the only black student in her class. Her favorite subjects were English and history, but Crystal had to work hard to pass her math classes. She was a little jealous that math was so easy for her older brother, Roy. He was also a good musician and later studied at the famous Juilliard School of Music.

One day Crystal's mother said, "Would you like me to teach you to play the organ and piano like Roy does?"

"I would like to learn to play," replied Crystal, "but I am not sure I want to spend all that time practicing. I would rather spend the time playing with my friends."

Her mother responded, "I know you may not like the lessons at first, but if you keep at it you will learn to like it. Later, you will enjoy playing for others at church, the way I do now. This little pump organ you will practice on came all the way from Groveland, Massachusetts, where I was born in 1851. I took it to Mississippi, then to Illinois, then to Kansas and finally here to California."

Later, Crystal inherited that strong oak pump organ – then passed it on to her own daughter. A century later that organ is a treasured heirloom in her daughter's present home, which is located on part of the same land Crystal settled on in 1890.

Crystal was in the first four-year class that started at the new Hollywood High School. When Crystal graduated from high school she asked her father, "Can I go on to college?"

Her father answered, "I would like for you to go but we just don't have enough money to send you now." So Crystal started working. She helped the family on the farm and earned some money at other jobs also. When she turned 21 Crystal's father asked her, "How would you like to homestead a farm of your own at Palmdale? You could apply for one near the farm I own there."

"Well," replied Crystal, "it is pretty hard work to develop a farm. I know how you struggled to get yours. Also that is a lonely place to live. ... But I am willing to try. It would be fun to own a farm of my own!"

Although it was back-breaking work, Crystal stuck at it for the three years needed to get her deed to the land. She got used to the rough work and the loneliness. Thankfully, her family came to visit and help out occasionally – even though it was a two-day trip by horse-drawn wagon or buckboard. But she suffered one big discouragement. Once, when she returned to her farm from a visit home, she found everything had been stolen. Her tools were gone. Her seed for new crops was gone. Even the many cans of fruit and vegetables she had put up in glass jars were gone. Still, she was thankful when she finally got the deed to her land.

It was through her piano playing that Crystal met her husband-to-be, Rufus Marshall. Rufus, a young black man, had left a hard life of discrimination in Texas. He found his way to California and settled in Santa Monica where Crystal met him when she was playing the organ and piano in a Santa Monica church – one of the several churches she served as organist or as church school teacher.

Crystal was pleased when Rufus asked her to marry him. Together they opened a successful catering business. During their following years together, Crystal and Rufus saw a building boom begin to develop in their area. Developers were buying up farm land and sub-dividing it into lots about 100 by 50 feet in size which they sold for $50 each. Crystal's father and mother bought several of those lots and Crystal and Rufus lived on one of them.

Crystal lived for 101 years – serving God and her neighbors from many racial backgrounds. When Crystal's Japanese friends were interned during World War II, she took care of their property until they were released. Crystal Albright Marshall is gone – but she is certainly not forgotten. Her loving spirit and good deeds live on through all the people she helped down through the years. As a pioneer black woman in California, her place in history is firmly established. Crystal taught us a great deal about how different races can learn to live together.

26

Lillian & Larry Driskill with Kazuko & Ted Esaki in front of his church

Ted Overcomes His Problem

When Ted Esaki was small he was very selfish. He would go to almost any extreme to get what he wanted. Young Ted didn't care if he was bad or if his behavior caused trouble for others as long as he could get what he was after.

When he was six he would do almost anything to get a candy bar. One day he thought, "I want a candy bar, but I don't have any money. I think I will try stealing one from our local grocery store. They won't miss one little candy bar—

besides, I am so smart I can hide the candy bar in my pocket and walk out of the store without anyone knowing I have it."

He got away with this stealing of candy bars for a while, but one day the storekeeper came around the corner just as he was putting the candy bar into his pocket. Ted thought, "He finally caught me, but he won't get my candy bar. I can still eat it if I stuff it into my mouth fast!" And that is what he did.

The storekeeper grabbed him by the arm and said, "Ted, I won't tell your parents about your stealing this time. But, if you ever do it again, I will tell them!"

Ted, from a Japanese-American family that were very strict, thought, "I don't want my parents to know about this. I won't steal any more candy bars here. I will do it another way. I will take money from my mom's purse and buy candy bars. If I take just a little change at a time she will never miss it. I can get away with it."

For a little while Ted got away with this new plan, but one day his mom caught him in the act. "So – you are the one who has been taking change from my purse! I knew someone was doing it but I didn't know if it was you or your brother or sister. When Dad gets home from work tonight we must talk about this."

His dad was unhappy, "Don't you know how wrong it is to steal things? You not only cause trouble by taking other people's property, but you also make us feel sad that our own son would steal from us – or from anyone. You will have to be punished. We must teach you not to do such selfish things."

"How will I be punished?" asked Ted.

"You won't be allowed to ride your bike for a week," replied his father. "And I also want you to know that – if you keep on stealing things – the city police will send you away to a reform school. There they will try to correct you, so you will stop doing bad things."

"Aw! No one would be mean enough to send a little kid away from home to such a reform school," scoffed Ted. "You are just trying to scare me."

"Come with me to the bus station," replied his father. "I want to teach you what could happen before it is too late."

At the bus station his father said, "See that bus there. It goes right by the reform school. I have seen a juvenile police officer escort teenagers onto that bus to take them to the reform school. Now, I am buying you a ticket on that bus. If you keep on stealing I will give the ticket to the juvenile officer and he will take you there."

Finally convinced, Ted wailed, "Please don't put me on that bus and take me away from home! I won't steal any more. I promise!" And he never did. But, as a reminder of what could happen, his dad tacked the bus ticket up on the wall in Ted's room. It stayed there for a long time. By looking at this reminder, Ted learned not to steal.

One of Ted's friends went to the church school at the Japanese-American Christian church in his hometown of Monterey, California. One day Ted decided to go with him. The church school teacher taught them this Bible verse, "All have sinned and fallen short of the glory of God" (Rm 3:23).

Ted asked the teacher, "Does that mean that everyone steals things, like candy bars and such?"

"No," replied his teacher. "Some people don't steal, but we are all selfish and self-centered by nature. We all do bad things which displease God. Maybe we tell a lie and hurt someone or it might be we make God unhappy by refusing to love God and others. Anything that hurts God, or anyone else, is sin."

"Well, I used to steal candy bars—also money from my mom's purse," said Ted. "I feel very guilty about it. I told my mom and dad I'm sorry I stole things and I paid the storekeeper for the candy I stole from him, but I have never told God that I am sorry. Should I do that, too?"

"Yes, you should," answered his teacher. "Let me teach you another Bible verse that I think will help all of you when you do bad things. 'If we confess our sins, God is faithful and just and will forgive our sins and cleanse us from all unrighteousness (evil)' (1 Jn 1:9)."

"You mean I will be made clean and new if I tell God about it?" asked Ted.

"Yes," replied his teacher. "Would you like to ask God to forgive you now?"

"Do I have to pray in front of all these kids?" asked Ted, turning red with embarrassment.

"No," replied his teacher. "You can do it tonight, when you say your prayers before you go to bed. But don't forget!"

That night Ted prayed, "O God, forgive me for stealing things. Help me to know that it is wrong to cause trouble for the storekeeper and for my parents. Help me to overcome my selfishness and self-centeredness. Help me to do things that are good for other people and not just what I like to do. Help me to love you – and others."

After this prayer Ted felt a lot better. He felt that God, as well as his parents, had forgiven him. It was a big start in overcoming his self-centeredness.

Today Ted is the young pastor of a Japanese-American church in Hollywood, California. Now he uses most of his energy to serve others. Ted really loves God and his neighbors, just as Jesus said we all should do (Mt 22:37-40). Ted's church, founded by Japanese-Americans, is a loving church which welcomes people of all races so now there are Chinese, Hispanic, Afro-American and white members as well as many of Japanese descent.

Ted spends a lot of time working with the youth in his parish. Once one of the children asked, "Why do you spend so much time with us?" Ted answered, "Because I love you and I don't want you to make the same mistakes I did as a child."

Now Ted gets great joy knowing he is helping others to overcome their self-serving attitude – just as he had to as a little boy. Don't you think all of us, young and old, could benefit from Ted's experience?

27

A Poem for Grandma

"What's the telegram about, Mom?" asked young Melody Smith. She could tell by the look on her mother's face that it must be bad news.

"Grandma is in the hospital with a heart attack" replied her mother. "She seems to be getting better. The doctors think she will be all right for a while – unless she has another attack."

Thankfully, they were home on furlough in New Zealand near their grandma when this happened. Leaving their vacation spot, they drove to the hospital as fast as they could. Grandma was in a lot of pain but fortunately she began to improve. In three weeks Grandma was able to come home from the hospital. She had celebrated her seventy-first birthday the day after she entered the hospital.

Melody liked living in other countries where her father, Graeme Smith, did agricultural missionary work. He had started a big irrigation project in Gode, Ethiopia; had managed a large church-related farm in Zaire; and had also done work in Papua New Guinea.

While they were in Gode, Melody had a scary experience. Somali guerrillas attacked their mission station. Five-year-old Melody was hanging on to her mother's skirt when a guerrilla bullet went through her mother's leg. The bullet missed Melody by inches. Melody learned that missionary life can sometimes be dangerous.

Another problem with working overseas was that Melody and her sister and two brothers had to be away from their grandparents a lot. Melody was glad that they were on furlough when Grandma needed them during her hospital stay.

Grandma improved enough to enjoy a wonderful Christmas celebration with them before they had to go back to the mission field.

When they did return to the mission field, Grandma said, "Pray that the Lord will make my faith stronger – so I won't worry about having another heart attack." And she did seem to be more cheerful than she had been for many days.

But soon, far away from Grandma in Papua New Guinea, Melody started to worry: "What if Grandma does have another heart attack? What if I never get to see her again? What if ... What if ... ?"

One day Melody went to her mother and said, "I am going to write a poem to Grandma. I want her to have something from me that will remind her that I love her. I want her to know I am praying for her, even though I am far away."

This is the poem that Melody wrote:

> Here's a little note to say,
> I hope you have a brighter day.
> Here's a little message to shout,
> I hope God will take away your doubt.
> Here's a little word that says,
> I know God will hear your prayers.
> Here's a little song I sing—
> God is with you in everything.
> This last line you already know: I love you so.

The next June Melody's Grandma had another heart attack and went to be with her Lord. But according to Melody's aunt those last days were happy days for Grandma. She was more cheerful and content than she had been in many years.

Do you think that one thing that helped Melody's grandma to be more cheerful was Melody's poem? Do you think you could write something to your grandma or some other relative, to cheer them up during a difficult time?

In May of each year we celebrate "Christian Family Week." But shouldn't every week be Christian family week? Like Melody, wouldn't you like to write a poem or letter to someone you love? Or, better yet, why not write to someone who has no one else to show love for them?

28

Elizabeth and Her Talking Birds

When Elizabeth Zook and her husband retired from serving as missionaries in Mexico they settled in California at a missionary retirement community. There she filled her life with teaching Bible classes, baking delicious homemade bread and trying to make life easier for her neighbors who were having problems getting out and about. But Elizabeth's most unique job was caring for her pet birds.

She started out with a gray and yellow cockatiel (a small parrot) named "Charlie" that Elizabeth taught to sing such songs as "My Darling Clementine" and "When the Saints Go Marching In." He was not perfect, but usually everyone could recognize the tune and most of the words – even when Charlie mixed them up.

Charlie's specialty was to whistle a duet with Elizabeth. This was a marching song which Elizabeth had learned in Mexico. Lifting his crested head high, Charlie proudly whistled his part. One day Charlie flew out the door of the new home and disappeared. Elizabeth theorized that Charlie flew off to Mexico to do missionary work there and she likes to think of him teaching Mexican children to sing: "Lord, I want to be in that number, when the saints go marching in."

Rather than pine too much for Charlie, Elizabeth next began to tutor "Pepe," a small blue parakeet, who learned even more hymn tunes than Charlie did. Soon neighbors could hear Pepe announce, "I am a Presbyterian" and then sing almost all of "Jesus loves me, this I know, for the Bible tells me so."

When Elizabeth's pastor heard him, he said, "That's pretty basic theology, for the Bible teaches that we are all sinners saved by God's grace. Pepe has become a good theologian (teacher of religion)."

When Elizabeth died, a member of her Bible class adopted Pepe. Perhaps Elizabeth is still smiling down – from her home in heaven – whenever Pepe mixes up and sings, "I am a Presbyterian scalawag, for the Bible tells me so."

29

Adventures in Thailand

Young Horace Ryburn was eleven when their church got a new pastor who had been a missionary to Siam (now Thailand). He loved to hold the Thai wood carvings of elephants and other animals that his pastor had brought back from that faraway country and wonder what it must be like to live there.

As the years passed Horace became more and more involved in the church – first as a leader in the youth program then as a delegate to various youth conferences throughout the area. Increasingly Horace became interested in serving the church, especially in some overseas mission work. After graduating from college, Horace enrolled in Princeton Seminary and during his first year there he took time off to visit the Board of Foreign Missions in New York City where he was examined, and accepted, as a missionary candidate for Thailand.

When Horace graduated from Princeton Seminary he had the highest grades in theology of anyone in his class and so was offered a one-year scholarship to study in Cambridge, England. By the time he finished his graduate study, it was 1938 and war was already starting in Europe. He came back to the U.S. to attend a missionary conference and make final preparations for going on to Thailand. At the conference Horace met Mary Turner, a Christian education specialist for the mission board who was one of the leaders of the conference. Horace was so impressed by her that he began courting her right away. By the end of the conference he knew this was the person he wanted to marry.

Even though Mary seemed ready to agree to his proposal of marriage, her family objected that it was too risky to marry a man she had known for such a short time and then go off with him to a foreign country. It was finally agreed that Horace would go on to Thailand and Mary would join him as soon as marriage plans could be worked out. Neither of them realized that the approaching war would keep them from seeing each other again for three years. However many love letters went back and forth across the ocean that separated them.

When Horace arrived in Thailand his first missionary job was teaching English and Bible at the mission school named "The Prince Royal's College" in Chiangmai. During his three years there Horace grew to love his job and his Thai students. Suddenly their tranquil life ended. On December 7, 1941, a shocking announcement came over the radio: "Japan has bombed Pearl Harbor. It is feared that missionaries in Thailand will be arrested and interned (made prisoners). Japanese soldiers started occupying Bangkok several days ago."

The next day word came that missionaries in Bangkok had already been imprisoned. It would only be a matter of time until the Americans in Chiangmai would face the same fate. Horace, with 14 other missionaries and two American businessmen, decided to try to escape across the border into Burma. At the border town of Mae Sai they were held by border guards until a powerful Thai friend came and got them released. All 17 of them escaped by foot across the small river that separated Thailand and Burma.

During their journey through the jungles they passed many timber workers who trained their work elephants to push over and carry the huge jungle trees. They were guided along the trails by Thai porters who knew the way and helped carry their baggage. Since paper money often loses value in wartime, the Americans had changed all their money to silver coins which were heavy and valuable, but not one of them was stolen during the entire escape journey.

Horace and Mary had a happy reunion when he arrived home. Finally they could complete their wedding plans. During the war they served a church in the U.S. and when it finally ended they returned to Horace's beloved Thailand in 1947 as a missionary couple. During his 38 years of missionary service Horace helped to develop 32 new churches in Thailand and helped in mission administration. Soon he became convinced that the church in Thailand would never be strong and secure until all church affairs were under the control of native Thai Christian leaders so he worked hard to make this transition. Finally in 1957 this happened and all the Presbyterian missionaries came under the care of the Church of Christ in Thailand.

Horace's close Thai friend and co-worker, Rev. Charoon Wichaiditya, helped to bring this about. He had faithfully cared for the church and mission affairs during the war and proved to be a spiritual leader for many years. Charoon was helped by other Thai leaders such as Elder Suty Gunanukorn who quietly contributed his church salary back into the church treasury because he and his wife had some income from rented houses that met their needs.

When Horace retired in 1976 Elder Suty wrote, "Everyone should so live that when present you are loved and trusted and when absent you are missed. Dr. Ryburn has so lived."

Over the years, Dr. Ryburn helped over a hundred Thai young people study at various schools and colleges in America. Some of these students became valuable church and government leaders in Thailand.

The next time you meet some missionaries, try to find out all you can about the country where they serve.

30

Francis Scott is the fourth from the left at a church meeting in China

Helping One Another

Francis Scott, a boy born to missionary parents in China, married Helen Rhodes, a girl born to missionary parents in Korea. After getting married, Francis and Helen themselves became missionaries serving in China during the difficult years of World War II. Francis worked in evangelistic areas helping some 30 Chinese pastors and evangelists over a ten-county area of Hunan, in south-central China, whereas Helen lent her musical talents helping with church choirs and women and children's ministry.

There were no auto roads in their rural and mountainous area of China so Francis had to walk many miles to the churches and chapels he served and usually he was away from home for two or three weeks at a time.

Once he visited a remote Christian village that had not been visited by a pastor for 13 years. He found them faithfully serving Christ and patiently waiting for a pastoral visit. Francis conducted the first communion service they had received in all those years and he examined and baptized several communicants who had prepared for his coming.

Another time while he was visiting a remote chapel he was surprised to hear a knock on the door of the room where he was lodging. Opening it, he found two Chinese soldiers who informed him their commander wanted him to come to his headquarters. Wondering what it was all about, Francis picked up his Chinese New Testament and followed the soldiers, who led him to a large open room where some 50 Chinese army officers were seated. At a sharp command from their leader they all stood at attention.

"Welcome, and thank you for coming," said the commander. "I am Colonel Liao, and these are my men. We heard that you are a teacher of the Jesus religion. We have heard good things about it, but my officers and I want to know more. I have invited you to come and tell us about this Jesus religion."

Francis thanked him and asked everyone to please be seated. He read a few verses from Colossians that contrast the old life of sin and evil-doing with the Christian new life of goodness, kindness and love. He told how God helps those who believe in Jesus to have changed hearts and lives: "Put off the old evil self ... and put on the new self ... as God's own people ... forgive as the Lord forgave you." (Col 3:9-13). Then he explained how God loved us so much that he sent his Son, Jesus Christ, to save us from sin and give us power to live this new life.

Francis then asked, "Do you believe that this is true?"

"Of course it's true!" shouted Colonel Liao. "Now, how do we become Christians?"

Francis gave Colonel Liao his Chinese New Testament and agreed to teach them if they would come to the chapel nearby. Every morning for the next ten days Colonel Liao and his second-in-command came to the chapel for study. At the end of the ten days Francis noted that Colonel Liao had carefully marked the entire New Testament that he had given him. Every night for Francis' public preaching service in the little chapel, Colonel Liao marched a whole company of his soldiers over to hear the preaching.

After their period of preparation, Colonel Liao and his second-in-command were baptized by Francis, with elders of the church assisting. When Francis had to leave them, Colonel Liao said, "In battle I have had bullets pass through my shirt, trousers and helmet, but I believe God kept me alive so I could meet you and become a Christian. I will try to be a good one."

During World War II everything became much more tense, even in this remote area, for there were battles being fought in the area. When the air-raid alarm sounded everyone was instructed to find cover. Francis had been taken very sick and was being treated at the Chenchow mission hospital. The doctors would not let him do anything for himself so the Christian male nurse, Mr. Liu, had to feed him, bathe him and even turn him over in bed.

Suddenly the alarm sounded, followed by the sound of approaching planes. Everyone was to hurry down to the bomb shelter in the basement of the hospital, but Francis knew he could not be moved. He was concerned to see that Mr. Liu continued to sit by his bed, reading a newspaper.

"Aren't you going down to the shelter?" asked Francis.

"Me?" replied Mr. Liu. "What for?" continuing to read his newspaper.

Only then did Francis notice his hands were shaking and

that he was holding the paper upside down! Mr. Liu was risking his life to show Christian love and loyalty to his patient.

When the Communists came to power in China, and mission work there was no longer possible, Francis and Helen began serving churches in America. One Sunday morning, while serving a church in Lancaster, Pennsylvania, Francis woke up and found that a huge snowstorm had piled up snow three feet deep! He lived a mile from the church, but he had promised to lead the worship service. All the other churches in town announced that services were canceled, but Francis, remembering how happy Chinese Christians were to see him walk into their remote regions, decided to go ahead.

He and his oldest son set out on foot for the church, and arrived to find almost a hundred other "Eskimos" had also gotten there somehow. Most of them were people who lived nearby. There, in the winter-wonderland God had created overnight, they held a joyful service of worship and one they would never forget.

Francis also served a church in Birmingham, Alabama, which had a unique outreach program, called the "Children's Fresh Air Farm." This summer camp program served 100 underprivileged children during June, another 100 in July and an additional 100 in August. Every year these 300 needy children were not only given free camping privileges but were also given free health care. Doctors and dentists from the church examined each child and gave them whatever care they needed. At Christmas time, each child's family received a box containing clothing, food and other gifts.

Years later many of the children said, "That camp was a turning point in my life. I learned that God loves me and you Christians cared about me. That made me decide to become a useful person, helping others in the same way I had been helped."

All of Francis' four brothers and sisters became missionaries to Asia. One sister, Betty Scott Stam, was killed by guerrillas in China.

Francis used the special talents God had given him to become a Christian leader, helping people in China and in America. How will you use the special talents God has given you? Like Francis, wouldn't you like to become a person who helps others?

31

Dr. Hail's "Almighty Turtle"

Alexander and Rachel Hail arrived in Japan in October 1878 – five years after the government's anti-Christian law had been changed. Still, after 200 years of opposition to Christianity, many Japanese people feared and hated Christians. In isolated areas you could still read signs that said: "Anyone disloyal enough to become a Christian can be punished by death."

Just three years before they arrived, a friend, Dr. James Ballagah, had been attacked and stoned by a mob when he preached near one of those anti-Christian signs at Mishima.

Dr. Hail's own missionary career almost ended in tragedy when he left the relative safety of the big city of Osaka to preach in the conservative town of Ise Yamada. He was attacked by rough young men shouting, "Chase out the foreigner! We don't want any 'Yaso Kyo' people here. ... Kill the foreigner!" And they started throwing stones at him.

Reporting this later, Dr. Hail said, "That was a scary experience. But I was happy to hear that one Christian lady there picked up one of the stones thrown at me and said, 'I'm going to save this stone and have it put in the foundation of the first church we build here in Yamada.' " (Later a church was built in Yamada – and that church sent out over 20 evangelists to help start churches in neighboring towns.)

It required bravery to keep up evangelistic work in spite of such opposition, but although it took some time for suspicious adults to come to love the Hails, Japanese children quickly gathered around, fascinated by these strange foreigners. Soon wherever Alexander went to preach, children would come running, shouting, "Here comes the Jesus man! Here comes the Jesus man!"

Dr. Hail had another problem: he found it very difficult to learn the Japanese language. There were few Japanese teachers who knew enough English to explain the meaning of Japanese words to him, but he finally found a young man, Komazo Kobata, who knew a little English and helped him to learn the language.

Even though he became one of Japan's most beloved and effective missionaries, Dr. Hail always had trouble pronouncing Japanese words. Most of his Japanese friends were too polite to correct him, but once someone decided it was best to let him know how he sounded to them and told him, "When you pray to God (*Kahmee*) it sounds to us like you are praying to a turtle (*kahmeh*). But we don't let it bother us because we know you mean 'God.' "

Dr. Hail laughed and said, "Thank you for telling me. I will try to improve." But he still couldn't get it right. For all of his many years of service in Japan, Dr. Hail kept praying to "Almighty Turtle." But his deep spirit of love for God and for people shone through so clearly – in his prayers and in his life – that his language mistakes didn't matter. Later, a Japanese friend said, "I felt relieved to find that the saintly Dr. Hail was human after all."

Because he did not give up – in spite of opposition, danger and language problems – Dr. Hail was a faithful servant in Japan for 45 years. During this time he helped to develop more than seven churches and two schools.

Rachel Hail shared her husband's missionary spirit and contributed greatly to the mission work in Japan as well as raising their children, John and Annie. Years later their son, John Eugene, who himself had served as a missionary for 14 years, died tragically when he was hit by chunks of flaming rock. He was climbing Mount Asama when suddenly the volcano erupted just as he was about to reach the summit.

Many people remember Dr. Hail's faithful missionary service in Japan. President Kinnosuke Morita of Osaka Girls' School tells of Dr. Hail's unflagging devotion to the Japanese people even at age 79. During the last three weeks of his life, President Morita recalls, "I saw Hail *Sensei* fall to the floor when he brought a book to put in our school library. When I helped him to get back up on his feet he kept saying, 'Don't worry, I'm all right, ... I'm all right, ... I have to go to the Leprosy Hospital to visit some leprosy patients there. ... I will be all right.' "

President Morita added, "I sent a student along with him

to make sure that Hail *Sensei* got safely to the Umeda train station. He was determined to go to help those leprosy patients in spite of his obvious weakness. He had baptized twelve leprosy patients there in 1912 and faithfully visited them. Hail *Sensei* was always thinking more about helping others than about protecting his own health."

Knowing the joy of having God's unconditional love brightened his own life and Dr. Hail wanted to share that love and joy with others.

His daughter, Annie Hail Hoekje, was by his side in Osaka, Japan, during the last hours of his life on June 5, 1923. Annie reported, "A few hours before he died my father said, 'Beautiful ... beautiful ... The Lord's glory is shining all around us. ... The Lord's glory is shining *in* us.' Then in a small voice he added, 'The Lord's glory shines in the Lord.' Father's spirit was wonderfully wrapped up in the Lord's glory. He had his Hebrew Bible open on his bed at Psalm 107:1, where it says, 'Give thanks to the Lord for he is good; his love endures forever.' "

Dr. Hail received many honors, including a cherished letter from the empress of Japan thanking him for his service as a Red Cross worker in Osaka hospitals during the Russo-Japanese War of 1904-1905. Even more did he treasure his living memorials: the churches and schools he started and the Japanese people he led to Christ.

The school, Osaka Jo Gakuin, has dedicated Hail Chapel as a memorial to Dr. Hail and his "missionary spirit." He might have always called God the "Almighty Turtle" but the Japanese church community appreciated how he and his family gave their lives in service to the Japanese people.

32

Father of the Ainu

When John Batchelor was still in grade school, he became fascinated with the stories he heard of mission work in foreign lands. He decided he wanted to go to China as a missionary.

With the support of his parents and his local church, he went to study at a seminary in Hong Kong. He did well in his studies of the Bible and the Chinese language, but the hot, muggy climate of Hong Kong made him sick.

His mission doctor said, "Perhaps you should change your plans and go to our mission station in the cold northern part of Japan. That Hakodate climate should be good for you, and with your long legs, you could walk through the snow drifts just fine!"

Soon after arriving in Hakodate, John met an Ainu man.

John was surprised because this Ainu didn't look like the other Japanese he had met. He had wavy hair, blue eyes and skin much lighter than that of most Japanese. Also he had a short, sturdy body and a bushy beard.

Finally John sought out a Japanese scholar and asked, "Who are these Ainu people?"

"The Ainu," replied the scholar, "were the first people to live in Japan. They occupied all of the main islands before other Japanese people came from the outside and took over their land—much like in South and North America where native Americans were pushed from their lands."

John decided to do missionary work with the Ainu, which meant he not only had to learn the Japanese language, but also the Ainu language, which was different from the Japanese. There were no railways or automobiles in Hokkaido when John began his work with the Ainu in 1879 so he usually rode a horse to visit the isolated Ainu villages. Sometimes he had to walk many miles over snowy roads to reach these people.

Since the Ainu language had never been written down, John decided to make an Ainu dictionary. Among the many people who helped him with this dictionary was a friendly Ainu chief, Penryuku. In June 1889, John published the first Ainu dictionary, containing 20,000 Ainu words translated into English and Japanese.

In the following years, John published over 40 books and articles. He eventually translated the Bible and many hymns in the Ainu language and also published many English and Japanese articles about Ainu folklore. Many of these people became Christians and John baptized over 1,000 Ainu converts. He was tireless in telling them that God loved them and sent Jesus to save them. The Ainu loved him, and many, like Chief Penryuku, became close friends and coworkers.

John was not only an evangelist but also a social worker bringing better health care to the Ainu. Seeing they had many health problems, especially tuberculosis, John said to his wife Louisa, "Let's build a health clinic next to our own house." Louisa agreed and the clinic was built in 1892. In the following years, over 2,000 Ainu were treated at this clinic. Later a Japanese Christian doctor joined in the Ainu hospital work.

In order to provide more education for the Ainu than they could get in their villages, John also was determined to build a special school for them. He went to an influential Japanese friend, Marquis Yoshichika Tokugawa, and said, "I know you are a friend of the Ainu people. Will you help me to raise at least ¥30,000 to start a school for the Ainu?"

"Yes, I will be glad to help," answered Marquis Tokugawa. "I am ashamed that our Japanese government does so little to help the Ainu. Let's build that special school. Education is the best hope for the future of the Ainu people."

In 1931, the school began its good work with Ainu students. John recruited Christian teachers from cooperating churches in Hokkaido.

John served the Ainu people for 60 years. Throughout Japan he was known as the "Father of the Ainu." After his death in England in 1944, John's former home in Sapporo was turned into an Ainu museum. It is located at the University of Hokkaido in Sapporo and is still used for Ainu studies at that university.

33

A Challenge for Sarah

A friend in Sarah Smith's hometown of Elmira, New York, asked her, "Why do you want to go to Japan as a missionary?"

"One reason," answered Sarah, "is the teaching and example of my pastor friend, Rev. G. W. Knox, who served so faithfully in Japan. The other is my older brother's sudden death while preaching one of his first sermons as a new pastor. One day, while feeling very sad about his death, I started reading my Bible. Suddenly the word 'Go into all the world and preach the good news to all creation' (Mk 16:15) leapt off the page. I felt God was speaking directly to me, telling me to go to Japan."

Before going to Japan Sarah had already taught several years at a special school for sick and handicapped children. In August of 1880 she sailed for Japan. Pastor Knox sent her off with his blessing and his greetings to old friends in Japan.

It took six weeks in those days to reach Japan, but soon Sarah Smith felt she was beginning to fulfill her lost brother's Christian mission. In spite of some health problems, she was very happy.

At first she taught at the Shin-ei Girls' High School in Tokyo. Then, after her mission board heard of her health problems they wrote saying, "Due to your health problems we want you to come home. Mission work is too hard for you, and we can't protect your health in that distant land."

Sarah wrote back, "I did not come to Japan to give up so easily. If you can't support my staying here I will find a way to support myself. I will go to Japan's pioneer island of Hokkaido. It is cold and snowy and not many people are willing to endure the rough life there. I can easily find a good teaching job there and I can stand the snow and cold because I grew up in the cold climate of upper New York state."

So to remain in her beloved Japan, Sarah moved to Hokkaido's port city of Hakodate in 1883. For several years she taught English, Bible and sewing classes at a local church. Then she said to a teacher friend, "Life in this port city is not interesting enough for me. I want to go into the very heart of Hokkaido and try the challenge of living and serving in the pioneer city of Sapporo. I hear the population there is only 18,000 and life is like it used to be in our American 'wild west.' "

Sarah got a job teaching at the government Boys' Normal School in Sapporo in 1887. Feeling she could start her own girls' school there she took seven of her Hakodate students with her and rented a barn from the Hokkaido government and converted it into two small classrooms. She had these first seven students live with her in her rented home. Thus began Sapporo's first girls' school.

Sarah said to her first students, "Don't you think it is interesting that our new school was born in a stable, just like our Lord Jesus?" Later she named the school Hokusei (North Star) after the star that led the wise men to where Jesus was born in Bethlehem. Later, to inspire the girls, Principal Tokito gave the school a motto: "Shine like stars in a dark world."

One of her first students, Michi Kawai, proved to be very special. Along with her and the other six dormitory students, 32 more joined the school as day students. Hokusei began to grow. With three Japanese teachers helping, Sarah provided classes in math, science, music, sewing, Japanese, English and Bible. This curriculum took six years to complete, with classes continuing ten months of the year. The special student, Michi Kawai, later became a famous Christian teacher who founded the highly respected school of Keisen in Tokyo. Like Sarah, Michi liked flowers and started horticultural classes at Keisen, the first such classes for women in all of Japan.

Sarah believed that good education must include the development of the whole person—body, mind and spirit. She said, "The fundamental idea of a school is to educate in the various branches of useful knowledge and thus fit the pupils for the duties and responsibilities of active life. The religious and spiritual influence brought to bear on the pupils is most important." From the beginning Sarah followed these ideas in her teaching.

There are many stories about Sarah's hard work, love for her students and constant efforts to help them develop a healthy body, mind and spirit. She was always concerned that her Christian students would be corrupted by the non-Christian festivals that went on around them. One day a student saw her closing the window blinds in the middle of the day. "Why are you doing that, *Sensei* (Teacher)," she asked?

"Because," answered Sarah, "today is the Sapporo Matsuri (Festival) and I don't want you girls to be harmed by the un-Christian things you might see."

Sarah kept such high educational standards for her Hokusei Jo Gakko Girls' School that eventually all departments of the their school system earned government approval, which made it possible for Hokusei students to go on to higher level government schools. Knowing this, more good students began applying to enter Hokusei.

Along with high educational standards, Sarah was determined to develop the Christian character of the school as much as possible. Worship services were held daily along with regular Bible study and prayer meetings. On Sundays, students were not forced to go to church services but they knew that Sarah expected them to go because she felt it was an essential part of their personal development.

Building on Sarah's good foundation, Hokusei now includes a girls' junior high school, two girls' high schools, two coeducational high schools, a junior college and a coeducational university located on four campuses. All these are part of today's Hokusei Gakuen's student body of over 7,000 students.

Although some of her students, and a few teachers, complained that Sarah was too moralistic and strict, they all respected her. One former student, Take Kondo, said, "Sarah Smith showed her concern and love for us by making us study hard, act morally and truly seek to serve our Creator God and the people around us."

Officially, Sarah served for 40 years in Japan, retiring from Hokusei in 1921. But since she stayed on as an adviser to Hokusei for another decade, Sarah really served in Japan for 50 years, finally returning to America in 1931 where she was active in the Japanese-American church in Pasadena.

In Japan Sarah's greatest public honor came when she was awarded the Sixth Order of The Sacred Treasure by the emperor and government of Japan in 1923 for her "meritorious services in the field of women's education" in Japan.

Amazingly, this strong woman missionary had the courage to go to the rough pioneer land of Hokkaido when even most Japanese people believed it was too cold and snowbound for people to live there. Having been ordered to come home by her mission board due to "poor health" she proved able to serve in Japan for 50 years and found the thriving school of Hokusei Gakuen.

Sarah Smith lived to be age 96 and her students still honor her by "shining like stars in a dark world."

34

Hokusei's devoted teachers – Alice Monk, Sarah Smith & Betty Evans (l-r)

Alice Goes to Japan's Siberia

Alice Maude Monk, who served as a missionary teacher for 36 years at Hokusei Jo Gakko Girls' School in Japan, began her life on the other side of the globe in Onawa, Iowa. Born on March 14, 1872 she was the oldest of four girls. When she was seven, her family moved to Chicago where she graduated from Jefferson High School. There she was sometimes teased about her "Monk" name which the dictionary says means a "a man who lives in a religious monastery." One day she was walking past a group of boys in the school hallway and heard one say, "For a monk, Alice is quite pretty, isn't she?" She soon learned that if she ignored them the boys would stop teasing her.

After she graduated from college, she taught in public schools in Chicago and in Aspen, Colorado, while continuing with her graduate studies. She then went for a year to work at the YWCA in Rochester, New York. While she was there Alice heard about suffering people in Japan and felt God was calling her to missionary service there.

Alice sent in her application and soon received an appointment as a missionary in Japan assigned to teach English and Bible at Tokyo Joshi Gakuin (Tokyo Girls' Academy). In 1904 at the age of 31, she sailed for the exotic land of Japan where she quickly earned her reputation as a scholar and leader.

After she had been teaching at Tokyo Joshi Gakuin for a year, her Mission Office in Tokyo received an urgent request from Sarah Smith, founder of Hokusei Jo Gakko Girls' School, which said, "Please send Miss Monk to help us here. We have just lost two missionary teachers. Miss Lillian Wells and Miss Mary Sherman have both left due to the cold climate here in Sapporo which has caused throat problems for them. Please send Miss Monk, or someone, as soon as possible. My own health is not good."

Joshi Gakuin was not happy to lose such a good teacher, but the mission leaders decided the greater need was at Hokusei. Everyone knew that Miss Sarah Smith was suffering from rheumatism and needed help so Alice moved to Hokusei in November of 1905.

When Alice arrived, Sarah Smith said, "Welcome to Japan's 'Siberia.' Life is cold and rough here but you are desperately needed. You are a lifesaver for me."

Alice found that life in those early days in Sapporo was

much like the "Pioneer West" in America for those who first settled America's West and the Japanese early immigrants who first landed in Hokkaido had much in common. There were few modern conveniences, little protection against the freezing cold in the winter and inadequate heat in the homes or in the classrooms.

Alice also found that the new school was struggling under the burden of not enough classrooms, too few good teachers and no funding to permit growth. Instead of giving up and going back to the easier life in Tokyo, Alice, like Sarah Smith, had a fighting spirit. She accepted the challenge of helping Hokusei develop into the thriving school both women wanted it to become.

"What are some of the problems you have with the students here?" Alice asked Sarah.

"We always lose a few students to the young men who fall in love with our attractive maidens," replied Sarah. "And we had eight girls go out on strike here complaining wqe were too strict in our grading and class discipline, but we soon resolved our differences and they returned to their studies. You will find life is never dull here."

In 1915 Sarah came to Alice and said, "My rheumatism is making it impossible for me to carry on a full schedule. Please take over my job as principal. I will continue to advise and help you in every way I can."

Thus Alice began her career as principal, which lasted for the next 24 years. At the end of her career, a missionary colleague, Virginia Mackenzie, said, "Alice Monk was not only an upright, dignified lady; she was the best scholar of any of the early missionaries who served at Hokusei. She was also a skillful pianist who played the piano for various groups in Japan."

A report on Hokusei that Alice wrote in 1929 says, "The

average attendance of students when I came here was about 130. Now it is up to 330. And Sapporo, which had a population of only 18,000 when the school began now has 158,000. I am optimistic about the future of Hokusei."

Among the outstanding students who passed through Hokusei portals during Alice Monk's tenure were Masa Inoue, who has served on the Hokusei board of directors for 20 years; Yoshiko Minami, who became the woman pastor of two churches and then returned to Hokusei to become head teacher in the Bible department of the junior and senior high school; and the much beloved Masae Nishioka, who was a successful evangelist in Tokyo before returning to Hokusei as the head teacher of the junior high Bible department.

When Alice's former students were asked what they liked about Miss Monk one said, "Miss Monk would encourage even the poorest, slowest students. She would keep repeating 'Try once more. Try once more. Try once more.' " Another added, "Monk *Kocho* (principal) would challenge graduating students to keep struggling for a better life. She would say, 'Girls, keep climbing higher, higher, ever higher.' "

"Monk *Kocho* was always trying to make us see that women could be good, strong leaders in society," interjected another student. "She would say, 'Women may be physically weaker than men but women are often stronger than men in other ways. They are often stronger in character, in terms of patience and endurance of hardships and trials. Just look at the example of Mary Lyon who started the first school for girls in America in 1837. We know it now as the famous Mount Holyoke College in Massachusetts; or the example of Umeko Tsuda who started the well-known Tsuda Women's College in Tokyo. These two women overcame many hardships to get these schools for women started."

Still another student added, "Monk *Kocho* would often say to us, 'Never say women are weak' or 'That is too difficult for me' or 'I can't do that.' Instead she encouraged us, 'Take a positive attitude towards yourself and you may be surprised at what you can do.' "

Alice Monk deeply loved her students and made that clear when she said, "Live in love and die in love. If you shine like stars in a dark world, your light will break through the darkness and bring light to others."

Although she was quite dignified, Alice Monk was also blessed with the ability to laugh at herself. Once a missionary colleague, the Rev. John Coventry Smith, was visiting. Not knowing he hated eggs "sunny-side-up," she served him that for breakfast. Unconsciously expressing his displeasure, John jabbed his fork viciously into the soft yellow dome. The soupy yellow egg yolk squirted across the table into the eyes of the stately Miss Monk.

There was a shocked silence. As John began to apologize profusely, Alice started laughing and said, "I know my gray eyes have flecks of brown in them, but this is the first time they have had yellow spots in them." And she carefully wiped each eye.

Eventually Alice Monk was forced to go back to America by the gathering storm of World War II, which began to cast a dark shadow over Hokusei in 1940 and 1941. Knowing the dangers involved for everyone, Alice and the other missionaries consulted with the Japanese leaders of Hokusei and together decided that for the sake of the missionaries and for the sake of the school they should probably leave.

Before that could happen, on August 17, 1941 the Japanese president of the board of trustees and the Japanese principal of the school came to call and advised Alice and the other missionaries to leave as soon as possible. Because of the uncertain situation, it was hard to find room on any ship. After a month of delays the only manner they could find to return to America was a roundabout way. Finally Alice and the other missionaries said "good-bye" to Hokusei friends and took passage on a ship out of Nagasaki going to Shanghai, China. After another month's delay there, they found a French ship which would take them to Manila in the Philippines. There several of the younger missionaries agreed to stay and teach at Silliman University in Dumaguete.

Alice, already 68, was past retirement age so she kept on and found a berth on the ship *President Coolidge,* which landed her back in the USA on Christmas Day, 1941, just 18 days after the Japanese attack on Pearl Harbor. If war clouds had not forced Alice to leave, no doubt she would have stayed at her beloved Hokusei even longer.

Settling down in Washington, DC, Alice kept speaking in churches as long as her health would allow. Finally, after a long battle with Parkinson's disease, she died in 1952 at age 79.

Alice would be proud to know that Hokusei has grown from the school of 526 students she left in 1941 to the large Hokusei Gakuen School System today which has six schools in four locations with over 7,000 students. This is quite a memorial both to Alice Monk, who helped to develop the school, and also Sarah Smith, the founder. The best memorial to these dedicated missionaries is their students – some of whom are still "shining like stars in a dark world."

35

Betty Teaches Through Love

Young Elizabeth Margaret Evans was raised in Minneapolis, Minnesota, where her father was a pastor. When Betty turned twelve her father took an assignment as a "home missionary" at the Sioux Indian Home Mission Station in South Dakota so Betty spent her teenage years there. She enjoyed here life there and when she finished school she herself taught at the Good Will Mission for Indians for three years. Finally in 1911, when she was 25, she was appointed a missionary to Japan.

Soon after arriving in Yokohama, Japan, Betty was sent to cold, snowy Sapporo in Hokkaido where she realized her childhood dream to be a missionary teacher at the North Star Girls' School, now known as Hokusei Gakuen. There she taught English and Bible classes and also helped with administration tasks. Betty loved to play volleyball and go with her students to the wonderful ski slopes nearby. In the winter they could put on skis at the school gate and be gliding down the nearby slopes in half an hour.

Betty was also asked to teach in several Sunday schools and the Kita-Ichijo Church where she worshipped (and which was at one time the largest Protestant church in Japan). Through the years she was so dearly loved and respected by her students and fellow teachers that one of her students, Yoshida Masako, who now teaches at Hokusei, compiled a book about her which records many words of praise for Betty written by former students. Maki Sasaki said, "Evans *Sensei* radiated love which sprang from her deep faith in God." Mie Funabashi added, "Evans *Sensei* not only taught God's love in Jesus Christ, but she lived it out in her relationship to me and other students with her wonderful Christian spirit." What impressed Ai Shimada was that "Evans *Sensei* taught me what unconditional love is like." Kazuko Machida added, "What still lives in my memory of Evans *Sensei* is the deep meaning of her prayers. I am still grateful for having learned from her and benefitted from her prayerful spirit."

Betty was on furlough in America when war broke out with Japan and for a while she was unable to continue teaching at her beloved Hokusei. She did keep up her work with people of Japanese ancestry by visiting the Japanese-Americans who were interned in camps in America and comforting many suffering people during that tragic time of confinement. This was not popular with some anti-Japanese people, but Betty knew it was what God wanted her to do—and it was *right* to do.

When the war ended, Betty was the first missionary back in Sapporo. No other missionaries arrived for several months, but she had hurried back when she received a letter from the acting principal of Hokusei, the Rev. Rinzo Onomura, saying, "I was in prison pending my trial for three months; ... I had been charged with anti-militarism and being pro-America ... and then was sentenced to eight months' penal service. I appealed to the higher court and was fortunately found not guilty there. The case has been very troublesome to the Hokusei Girls' School and the Kita-Ichijo Church ... but now we can freely hold religious services in the Chapel every morning. *I hope you will soon come back to us. I shall expect you.*"

Hokusei's love and respect for Betty was shown by their welcome when she arrived back on Dec. 15, 1947. In a letter written to friends in America she described it: "About 100 were waiting on the railway platform—friends, alumnae and teachers. Some 200 girls waited beyond the gate, in the falling snow, while the rest of the girls were lined up in front of the school, blocks away. Many were laughing and crying at the same time as we shook hands and bowed. ... As I greeted the 850 girls in front of the school, I noticed their worn clothing. Many wore slacks fastened at the ankles for warmth and many were reinforced with patches. But, in spite of their poverty and poor clothing, their faces were beautiful." Betty added, "Gifts of scarce food and other things poured in. ... When I hesitated to accept so much they would say, 'You must eat a lot and keep well for we need you.' "

Betty was appointed principal of Hokusei upon her return in 1947 and continued in that leadership role until her retirement in 1951. Since the days when Sarah Smith founded the school, there has always been an emphasis on getting as many Christian teachers as possible and encouraging students to become Christians. Just before Sarah Smith retired she took Betty, then a young missionary, up a nearby mountainside which had a good view of the city and of Hokusei. Sarah said, "Betty, I have often come up here to pray for Sapporo and Hokusei. I would like to have you continue that."

Years later Betty described this request, "I felt that her mantle was falling on my shoulders and I promised to continue that custom." In a wonderful way Betty fulfilled her childhood dream for she served God and the Japanese people for 40 years, retiring in 1951. In 1957 Betty went back to Hokusei to take part in the 70th anniversary of the school. While there she was awarded the "Fifth Order of The Sacred Treasure" by the emperor and the government of Japan for her contribution to educational work in Japan. This was a great tribute to a wonderful missionary whose loving service still radiates through the lives of her beloved Hokusei students and friends.

36

Dot Taylor (3rd from l.) with Hokusei Gakuen friends.

Keeping Young in Japan

Dorothy Taylor was excited when she read in her church bulletin, "Missionary teachers are urgently needed for our Christian schools in Japan."

"I could do that," thought Dot. "I am a teacher and, although I am 41 years old, I think I could start a new career in Japan."

When she told her pastor she was interested, he said, "Oh Dot, that's not for you. We meant that for our young people."

Dot laughed and said, "Maybe teaching in Japan would help to keep me young."

In spite of her age, Dot was commissioned as a missionary to Japan in June 1949 and began preparations to go. She studied Japanese at the Yale Institute of Far Eastern Languages for a year and finally sailed for Japan in 1950. After more language study in Kyoto she began her teaching in Japan's cold, snowy city of Sapporo at Hokusei Gakuen.

When Dot arrived in Japan she had plenty of past teaching experience, for after she graduated from college she had taught in public schools for many years, pioneering as a teacher of the enrichment classes that were being developed at that time. She also helped create new teaching materials and then was assigned as the first woman teacher at Baltimore City College. She felt that with all this background, God had helped prepare her well to teach in Japan.

At Hokusei Dot's first assignment was to teach Bible and English classes for young women in junior high through junior college—a post she held for the next eleven years. In 1962 she was asked to teach in the newly developed coeducational four-year college program—which she did for the next eleven years.

When a friend asked how she endured the cold winters of Sapporo with its heavy snows, below zero temperatures and little heat, Dot smiled, "I would teach many classes with my ski pants and jacket on. That was the only way some of us could stay warm. But the snow did have one advantage: I was able to enjoy the famous life-size snow sculptures of animals, castles and other buildings at the annual Sapporo Snow Festival. As the years went by, we found better ways to heat our classrooms so we could dress more normally."

Dot loved her students and they loved and respected her, but some complained she was "too strict" and set "too high" standards for them to reach. Once a student asked, "Why are you so strict, *Sensei*?"

Dot replied, "I am strict because I want each one of you to do the best work you can. But I do try to be fair with you. All I ask is that you try hard and don't 'goof off' because when you are lazy you are wasting the talents God gave you."

Later Dot wrote in her "Hokusei College Memories," "Maybe I was too hard on some of the students with my over-zealously strict standards."

One student, Ko Kano, came to her special attention. Once someone told Dot, "There is a young girl named Ko who wants to enter the junior high department here but she doesn't have enough money. Her family can't afford to send her away to a boarding school like ours."

"I will see what I can do to find some help for her," answered Dot. She wrote to her home church, Hunting Ridge Church in Baltimore, Maryland, and asked, "Is there any group in the church that can provide a scholarship for a little girl who would like to enter our school?"

Soon a letter came back saying, "The people of our Sunday school have decided to sponsor that little girl, Ko Kano."

Ko not only finished junior high, but she went on to graduate from junior college in 1961. All went well with her until the days of the worldwide student rebellion. Ko became a leader of the rebels at Hokusei and said rude things to her teachers, cut classes and urged other students to go out on strike.

In spite of Ko's rebellious attitude and actions, Dot never gave up on her. Finally Ko came around and developed into a fine Christian leader in the school, in her church and in her community. Other teachers were surprised.

A lifelong friendship developed between Dot and Ko. Every Christmas Ko knitted a special gift for Dot and even after Dot retired, Ko managed to visit her in Baltimore. Dot said, "I'm glad I didn't give up on Ko when some said I should."

Looking back on her time in Japan, Dot said she retired from Japan with many happy memories: the fine friendships she developed while holding a Bible class in her home for more than 20 years; the fellowship from teaching Bible classes at the Hokko church and the Asabu church for seven years; and – on a lighter level – the school picnics held in beautiful locales like Shakotan Peninsula and Lake Shikotsu.

When asked about her most unhappy experience at Hokusei, Dot replied, "That would have to be the terrible fire we had in December of 1963. One night the fire alarms sounded and soon a horrible fire was quickly spreading from the second floor art rooms of the senior high on to the music room and the auditorium. It finally reached the second floor classrooms and faculty studies of the college. Since it was impossible to stop the fire, faculty and students rushed to rescue library books from the first floor, carrying them to relative safety in the high school's concrete building. I did what I could to help, but I felt so weak and helpless watching months of research notes and data of the faculty going up in smoke. It was awful!"

Dot added, "It seemed hard to believe how quickly the school recovered from the fire but within a month there were prefab classrooms and faculty studies ready for college classes at our new site, Oyachi, a suburb of Sapporo. This new 64-acre campus had fire-resistant concrete buildings thanks to a generous grant from the 'Fifty Million Fund' of the Presbyterian Church. The Webster Groves Presbyterian Church in St. Louis gave $100,000 because they had survived a tragic fire and were able to sympathize with us in our need. Of course, our Japanese friends also gave sacrificially and worked hard to give Hokusei a fine new start after the fire."

During her 23 years of service in Japan, Dot received several special honors including the "Fourth Order of the Sacred Treasure" by the emperor and government of Japan. But always Dot kept young in spirit. One sign of it was her bright, jolly laugh. A missionary colleague at Hokusei, Millie Brown, once said, "Dot's laugh sounds like that of someone half her age. Teaching in Japan has really kept her young."

When asked about her missionary call Dot said, "I think it can be summed up in the Bible verse: 'You did not choose me; I chose you and appointed you to go and bear much fruit, the kind of fruit that endures' " (Jn 15:16).

After Dot's death a missionary colleague wrote to her sister saying, "Dot did one fine job at Hokusei. She was a genuine credit to the school and to the church. I'm sure the Lord says to her, 'Well done, good and faithful servant. ... Enter into the joy of your Lord!' " (Mt 25:21).

37

Serving God in Japan

Grace Hereford was born in the exotic land of Japan in 1903. Growing up in the big city of Osaka, Grace didn't think of Japan as exotic or different. To her the beautiful kimonos that girls wore and the custom of taking off your shoes when you entered a house were only natural. Japan was her "home."

She knew her missionary parents were from a faraway country called "America" but until she was seven, she had never been there. Just before her first trip to the U.S. she was looking at an American magazine with a picture of a new invention. "What is that?" asked Grace.

Her mother answered, "That is a new automobile. It can run by its own engine and doesn't need horses to pull it."

"When I get to America on furlough I want to ride in one of those!" said Grace in an excited voice. And when she finally did, it was a great thrill.

When she was eleven, Grace came to their Japanese pastor and asked to join the Japanese church. When he asked her about her faith, she told him she believed in Jesus Christ as her Savior and knew that she needed God's love and forgiveness. She especially felt she needed forgiveness for an argument with her younger brother that almost resulted in his losing an eye.

At the time Grace was six years old and loved to play with her dolls. One day her four-year-old brother, Francis, came begging her to play with him. Grace was sitting above him on a big shelf with her dolls and wouldn't come down. He got so angry with her that he picked up his mother's sharp sewing scissors and threw them at her. The scissors didn't hit Grace but they fell back on Francis and cut him badly between the eyes. If they had fallen a little to the right or left they would have put out an eye. Receiving God's forgiveness for her part in this near-tragic accident was a great comfort to Grace.

In Japan Grace was taught at home by her mother until she was 14. Then she was sent alone to America to study at a college preparatory school for three years and then on for four years more to the university.

During her prep school days a friend asked Grace, "Do you plan to become a missionary like your parents?"

"No!" answered Grace hotly. "Everyone expects me to be a missionary, but I want to be different."

However in college Grace began to attend Student Volunteer Movement conferences with her friends and there she became interested in a missionary career. She thought, "My grandfather did a good job as a minister here in America and my parents were faithful missionaries to Japan. Maybe God is leading me to be a third generation Christian worker."

Learning that the mission school for girls in Osaka, Japan, (now Osaka Jo Gakuin) needed a music teacher as soon as possible, Grace agreed to go teach music there at the young age of 22. Having grown up in Japan, she knew the Japanese language on a child's level. Now she found that she had to study hard to upgrade her Japanese to an adult level.

After teaching music in Osaka for a year, Grace met a wonderful Christian Japanese teacher of music, Eizaburo Kioka, who had been converted in her father's Bible class. His family opposed his decision to become a Christian, but the Japanese church people, and now Grace, became his new "family."

Eizaburo was skilled in pipe organ teaching. Even though Grace had studied piano and the pump organ in school, now she took lessons in the more complicated pipe organ with this new teacher and friend. Another good friend for Grace in those early teaching days was the Japanese pastor of the East Church in Osaka—Shiro Shimokoshi.

Grace played the organ for his church services and also became good friends with his wife, Kikue. For a young girl far from her family and former friends, this pastor and his wife provided just the kind of love and support that Grace needed. Pastor Shimokoshi later died, but his widow still writes to Grace today.

In 1939 Grace was asked to play the organ for the German-speaking worship services in Kobe, Japan. There she met an interesting German missionary pastor by the name of Egon Hessel, who was the leader of the group. He was a widower with two small boys, five and four. His wife and a baby had died in childbirth.

Pastor Hessel asked Grace to teach piano to his two young boys. Soon their friendship blossomed into something more romantic. They were married the next year in Osaka on the Japanese Emperor's birthday. This is a holiday in Japan so they knew they would always have a vacation from work to celebrate their future wedding anniversaries.

Since he was a German and she an American, the complications of World War II required they leave Japan for America. Together they served the Presbyterian church in America until the end of the war when they again returned and took up their missionary service in Japan.

One of Grace's step-sons, Dieter Hessel, now serves at Princeton Seminary doing special studies. Grace's younger sister, Nannie, also became a missionary to Japan.

When Grace went back to Japan she found a music teacher who taught with her at Osaka Jo Gakuin had much in common. Yoshiko Ohta and Grace were born in the same year, in the same city, on the same street. Now they were teaching the same subject in the same school. Their friendship has continued, unbroken, for 65 years.

God has given Grace an interesting life of Christian service in Japan where she lived for 48 years and in the U.S. where she is now retired.

What plan do you think God may have for your life? Why not start thinking and praying about it now. Maybe God will reveal an interesting life plan for you, just as he revealed one to Grace Hereford Hessel.

38

Dorothy (1st on l. in front row) and Hokusei friends

The Unwanted Child

While Dorothy Schmidt was a young child her grown-up sister said, "You know you were born unplanned and unwanted in this family. We already have four grown children and we don't want a young child like you." From then on Dorothy really did feel unwanted and unloved.

It was not until she became an adult that she learned her name means "gift of God." Knowing this helped her gain a more positive image of herself. She thought, "If my name means 'gift of God' I must have great value in God's sight."

She liked to go to church school for there she learned that God really did love her. Her favorite Bible verse became "God so loved the world that he gave his only Son ... " (Jn 3:16). Often she would put her own name in the verse saying, "God so loved *Dorothy* that he gave ... ." This helped her to feel loved and wanted. Her favorite song was "Jesus Loves Me."

But when her church school teacher asked her to learn a lot of other verses Dorothy felt a little rebellious. "Why do we have to learn so many Bible verses when all we need to do is look in the Bible and read them?" she asked.

"Well, I can think of three reasons why you should learn Bible verses," answered her teacher. "It is a good way to learn more about God, about God's world and about yourself. Also learning verses is like 'eating spiritual food,' which will help you grow stronger spiritually. A third reason is that having key verses fixed in your memory could be helpful when you may face some crisis in your life."

Later, when Dorothy became a prisoner of war, these memory verses helped her so much she became very grateful that her teacher had helped her to learn them.

One happy moment in her life came when Dorothy learned from her history teacher that she was valedictorian (best student) in her high school graduating class. This meant that the Kiwanis Club would give her a two-year scholarship to Bloomsburg Normal School (teacher's college) in her home state of Pennsylvania. She was so happy and excited that she ran over a mile back home to tell her parents the good news. She felt crushed when her mother said, "You can't go to college. You have to go to work right away to help support the family."

So the scholarship for two years of free college went to the second highest student in her class, also a girl. But Dorothy didn't give up. She was determined to find some way to go to college. She took a job as secretary in a lawyer's office. But as she typed, the keys seemed to be saying, "I want to go to college! I want to go to college!"

After worrying for more than a month, Dorothy asked her former teacher, Miss McClellan, to talk to her mother about giving Dorothy her freedom to go to college. Her mother finally agreed saying, "You can go, but the family won't give you any help toward your college expenses."

Her teacher persuaded the Kiwanis Club to give her a partial scholarship for three months, with a promise to send some additional money every three months. Full support then came for her second year of college. Dorothy also took part-time typing jobs at the college to help with her expenses. She worked late every night and all day on Saturday, a schedule which left her little time to study and even less for the pleasures that most students enjoyed.

During her second year of college Dorothy became more involved in church work, teaching Sunday school at a nearby church. One day she heard a missionary speak about her work in India. She became interested in becoming a missionary and began to read books on missionary work including *Christ of the Indian Road* by E. Stanley Jones.

But it was her college teacher, Edna Hazen, who had the greatest influence on Dorothy's becoming a missionary. Miss Hazen confided to Dorothy that she wanted to become a missionary but was prevented from doing so by the sudden death of her brother. She had to go to work to help support her family. Miss Hazen said, "If you want to become a missionary, and will promise to do so, I will help you to complete your college studies and get your degree. If you really go to the mission field you won't have to pay back any of the money I provide for you."

In her third year, her college got Dorothy a job teaching fourth grade at Hatboro, Pennsylvania. This was close enough to Temple University for her to take additional classes there in the late afternoon and evening and finish four years of college.

After finishing college, with Miss Hazen's encouragement, Dorothy studied two years at the New York Biblical Seminary. Then in 1937 she received a mission appointment to Japan to teach at North Star Girls' School in cold Hokkaido where snow often stayed on the ground from early December until late in March.

Sometimes school could not start until the snow plows had cleared away the snow, which occasionally piled up as high as four or five feet. But there was also a plus side to the cold weather. Dorothy enjoyed the beautiful snow sculptures made for Sapporo's winter festival – snow carvings of full-size houses, castles, whales and animals that made Hokkaido famous as Japan's winter wonderland.

Dorothy had three years of teaching experience before she came to Japan. She was a good teacher, and her students liked her. To some students, who were facing difficult problems, she became like a big sister. By listening to their problems and counseling them, she gained some lifelong friends.

But soon hostility began to grow between Japan and America and Dorothy found that some Japanese people began to call her an "American spy." Finally, because of the growing danger, Dorothy had to leave Japan. She was assigned to teach at Silliman University in Dumaguete, Philippines. But soon thereafter Japan captured Dumaguete City and Dorothy, along with other American missionaries, was put in an internment camp.

Under the stress of prison life Dorothy saw people around her taking various attitudes. A few prisoners fell into defeatism. which led to despair, and often to mental illness or even death.

Others, the majority, approached their prison life with a stance of endurance. Often, with their minds set on the task of just surviving each day, these prisoners gradually became bitter, cynical people, filled with hatred and feelings of revenge or self-pity. Others, like Dorothy, assumed the positive attitude of trying to become better persons through this suffering.

For her part, Dorothy quietly recited hymns and Bible verses in her mind. She used her memory to relive happy times with her church and school friends, and she imagined doing these things again after being released from captivity. At first she prayed a lot but, as she grew weak from starvation, she found she didn't even have strength enough to pray. Yet even at the times of greatest weakness, the Bible verses she had learned as a child floated effortlessly up into her mind.

The verses which brought comfort and help to her included: "Come unto me, all who labor and are heavy laden, and I will give you rest" (Mt 11:28); "God is our refuge and strength, a very present help in trouble" (Ps 46:1); "We are more than conquerors through him who loved us" (Rm 8:37). She was glad her church school teacher had made her learn many Bible verses as a child for now when she desperately needed them, they were there!

While in prison, Dorothy wrote: "No matter what happens to me, whether I live or die, all is well. In all of my life's experiences since following Jesus Christ, I have found His strength adequate. He taught me not only how to live adventurously and abundantly, but also how to die courageously. Friends, I do not know anyone today who can give such strength and courage except the living God."

After recovering from her internment camp experiences, Dorothy returned to Japan. She resumed her teaching at North Star Girls' School in Sapporo, where she had taught before the

War. Her fellow teachers and the students welcomed her back.

In 1954 Dorothy was transferred to Tokyo. At first she taught at Meiji Gakuin University and then later went to Tokyo Women's College, where she stayed from 1968 until her retirement in 1974. In 1981 she revisited Japan to renew old ties and friendships.

She remembered with great joy her Japanese colleagues who had shown her so much friendship and appreciation. But Dorothy's longest and closest friendship in Japan was not with a student or another teacher, but with a Japanese lady named Yone Koike. *Yone-san,* which is what Dorothy calls her, lived in the same house with Dorothy as her friend and housekeeper for over 30 years. Recently Yone-san came to America to visit her old friend Dorothy in her retirement home.

A retired missionary friend of Dorothy's, Lillian Driskill, said, "It was the example of Dorothy's work in Japan, and her love for Japanese people, that led me to decide to go to Japan as a missionary." At age 84, Dorothy's health is not good but Lillian's praise of her work – and Dorothy's good memories of Japan – provide great comfort to Dorothy in her illness.

39

Woman Police Helicopter Pilot

"Teresa! Come down out of that tree," shouted her mother. "One of these days you're going to break your neck doing that. Why do you have to be such a tomboy?"

"I'm all right, Mom," called back active young Teresa Lincoln. "Besides, why should we let the boys have all the fun? I can climb trees just as well as they can."

Terry could do many things as well as boys could. She was a good bike rider, a good baseball player and she could outrun most of the boys in her neighborhood. She didn't know it at the time, but these "boyish" activities were helping Terry get ready for an exciting life as a woman police officer in Los Angeles, California.

When she first graduated from school, Terry took a very "lady-like" job as a secretary. But one morning on her way to work she heard an interesting announcement on her car radio: "The Los Angeles Police Department is looking for qualified women police officers, including possible helicopter pilots. If you think you may be qualified, please apply."

"That sounds a lot more exciting than being a secretary," thought Terry. "I think I'll go check out that job."

When her mother heard about it she said, "Oh no! Not again. Why do you always want to try dangerous things?"

But Terry was now a grown woman, with her own husband and home, and her mother knew she was free to do this if she wanted to – so she didn't interfere.

Terry was more afraid her husband might object. Imagine her pleasure when he said, "That sounds neat. Go for it!"

Although most of her other relatives and friends said, "You'll never make it," Terry did make it. She was accepted as a trainee, and began her training.

During her six months at the Police Academy, she found she could run the obstacle course and shoot firearms as well as the men could. This beautiful woman, with blonde hair and blue eyes, proved to be as tough as anyone in her class. She became one of about 1,000 women officers, along with 7,000 men, in the Los Angeles Police Department.

For the first five years on the police force she worked on street duty – in the dangerous downtown area of Los Angeles. Some days were pretty dull, with almost nothing to do but paperwork. Other days it looked like everything happened at once: robberies, gang fights and murders.

One day Terry and her police partner were called to investigate a gang fight going on downtown. Using their siren and flashing lights they drove their patrol car as fast as was safe. But when they got there it looked like the gang fight was over. Terry got out of the patrol car to check out one end of the street while her partner went to the other end.

Suddenly Terry was surrounded by several gang members with guns pointed at her. Praying, "God, help me keep my cool and talk my way out of this," she began reasoning with the gang members. "You guys know if you shoot me there will be hundreds of other police coming after you. My partner is just up the street and he will report everything."

Feeling that God was with her and helping her, she calmly walked up the street toward her partner and the patrol car. The gang members kept shouting dirty names at her but let her go. It was one of the most scary experiences Terry ever had.

On another similar occasion, her police partner was not able to get away alive. They were involved in a shoot-out with robbers holed up in a large warehouse. Terry's partner insisted she stay behind the patrol car and keep shooting—while he circled around to the back door. Somehow he got through the back door, but there was a wild shoot-out inside the warehouse during which Terry's partner was killed. Other police arrived and the robbers were arrested, but it was too late for her partner. Terry was saddened, not only because she lost a partner, but also because she felt he had died trying to protect her—by deliberately taking the most dangerous job.

When she became eligible, Terry applied for training as a helicopter pilot and became one of only two women helicopter police in an air support team of about 100—the largest air support police team in the world. Although she is in training to pilot the mighty "Astar" helicopter, Terry has already been piloting the "Jet Ranger" helicopter for over two years. She spends about five hours in the air – in two separate shifts each day – on her duty days.

Her helicopter is equipped with "Gyroscope Binoculars" powerful enough to read a car's license plate numbers from 500 feet in the air. Seeing a thief go through a window, she can radio a patrol car on the ground telling them what color shirt the thief has on or what kind of sneakers are being worn.

She also has a video camera which can record what is going on as a thief runs through back yards along with an "Observer" on board who helps to report these things. At night she has a powerful spotlight that can search out a running criminal in the darkest streets or alleys.

Her advice to people on the ground is: "When you see a helicopter spotlight from above, know that there is a criminal loose in your area. To protect yourself, turn off your inside lights and turn on all outside lights. This way the criminal can't see to come into your home and attack you." Another piece of advice is, "Make sure your house has a street number that can be seen from above – on the curb is O.K. but on the roof would be better. That way we can tell the patrol car where we see trouble brewing. It could save your life."

One day Terry's helicopter got lost in heavy clouds so she couldn't find her way out. Determined not to panic, she prayed, "Lord, help me keep calm and use my instruments correctly. Help me not to crash into a mountain or a tall building." With God's help, she kept her mind clear – eventually finding her way out before running out of gas. That was almost as scary as the time she had to talk her way out of being killed by gang members.

One day Terry was doing volunteer work at her church in La Puente. Seeing her good work a man said, "Have you ever considered going into Christian work?"

"I feel I'm already doing one type of Christian service," replied Terry. "I am using the talents God gave me to help keep our area safe. Besides, I do a lot of good by helping people on drugs get into a rehabilitation program – when drugs are involved in their arrest. I can't force it on them, but when they ask me about my Christian faith I can share it with them."

Terry added, "Helping victims of crime is another thing I find a lot of meaning and joy in doing. When a victim gives me the right information and I solve the crime, I always tell them 'You helped me to solve it.' This not only makes them feel good, it also helps them to get over the trauma of having been robbed or attacked."

Using her God-given talents, don't you think that Teresa Lincoln McIntosh is glorifying God in her own unique way? Although she is not doing what we usually mean by "church vocation," shouldn't we recognize that what she does is an important form of community service?

40

Genevieve, Content at 102

Genevieve Compton, 102, greeted me with a smile. "Come in," she sang out, her blue eyes sparkling a warm welcome.

I was curious concerning Genevieve's secret of long life and asked when she first came to live at Westminster Gardens.

"Well," replied Genevieve, "after living in retirement in Long Beach, California, for about 20 years, I moved here ten years ago when I was 92. For the first five years I lived independently and then because I needed help with my medication and couldn't walk well, I moved here to the Health Center. The nurses and others are very good to me."

"How is your health now?" I asked.

"Good," she replied, "but when I was 90 I almost died. I did a very foolish thing. I was taking my handful of pills every morning with only a half cup of coffee. The result was that I 'blew out' my stomach and developed severe ulcers. My doctor was shocked I didn't know enough to drink a lot of liquids with my medication, but by God's grace I got well again."

"Have you had any other problems?" I inquired.

"When I was 98 I had a stroke. My mind became so addled I thought I had lost my marbles for sure. But, again, God performed a miracle and healed me. It was an answer to my desperate prayers that God would clear up that terrible confusion I felt in my mind and the weakness that crippled my body. I feel completely healed now."

Seeing how well she could hear me, how clearly and brightly she talked and how charming she looked, with curly white hair and only slightly stooped shoulders, I agreed. She looked at least 20 years younger than her actual age. "You must have seen a lot of changes in the past 102 years," I observed.

"I certainly have. I was born in Los Angeles in 1891," answered Genevieve. "When I was seven, my mother died, leaving three little girls. Her two maiden sisters and Grandma took us to raise. In those days Los Angeles was small and San Francisco looked down on us calling us 'that small Mexican town in Southern California.' In spite of the loss of my mother, my childhood was happy. Being in a Christian home meant my life was full of church, Sunday school and music – which I loved. Unlike some kids, I also enjoyed school and was eager to learn. I liked being with people – and still do.

"I have lived most of my life in this area and am one of those rare birds, a native Californian. When I was 23 I married a minister who was 28 years older than I, but in good health. We had ten wonderful years together before he died of a stroke. I always felt a part of his Christian ministry and we served a 'home mission' church in Southwest Los Angeles for seven years before he retired."

"What did you do after your husband died?" I asked.

"Lots of things," replied Genevieve. "I was the recording secretary for the Women's Christian Temperance Union; I was a companion to elderly people and did practical nursing; also I worked with the Long Beach Union Rescue Mission – and of course always worked in the churches where I attended.

"I taught Sunday school classes, sang in choirs and was a leader in women's missionary societies. Even now at age 102 I get around in this wheelchair to visit other patients here in the Health Center – and try to cheer them up."

"You amaze me!" I said. "What word could I use to describe your life here? Could I say 'happy' or 'content'?"

"You may say both of those," exclaimed Genevieve. "I am happy and I am content. However, there is one thing that bothers me. When I look at TV or read the newspapers I am appalled at how cruel people can be to each other in the world today. Everywhere violence seems to be a common response to problems—here in the USA. And cruel wars are going on in Bosnia, Somalia and other places around the world. I don't understand why people everywhere can't enjoy the good, peaceful life I have here in these beautiful gardens, surrounded by flowers and good, friendly people."

"Now that you are over 100 do people tend to get more excited about your birthdays?" I asked.

"They really do. For the past four years I have been invited to a nearby elementary school on my birthday. It began when I was age 99 and the kindergarten children there oohed and aahed at seeing someone almost 100 years old. Two teachers placed a crown on my head saying, 'We crown you our One Hundred Day Queen, for this is our 100th day in school for our kindergarten children.'

"After the party one little boy ran up and hugged me. Soon all the others followed. They were beautiful children and their sweet hugs were so natural. I'll never forget that moment."

"Are you ever concerned about how soon God will be calling you to your eternal home in heaven?" I asked.

"Oh no!" said Genevieve cheerfully. "I don't worry at all. That is up to the Lord. Every morning I say a prayer of thanks that God has given me another day. I have had a good life and I am at peace with God, with those around me and with myself. I am ready anytime."

After holding her strong, steady hands for a closing prayer I thought, "If I could be like Genevieve, maybe living to be 100 might not be so bad, after all."

41

Healthy at Age 102

Aside from his white hair and hunched shoulders, Dr. Ralph Stewart did not appear to be 102 years old. He looked healthy. He was seated in his recliner, surrounded by magazines and newspapers.

"What do you like to read?" I asked.

"Everything!" he answered. "Everything from Christian Century to magazines on botany and zoology. I still subscribe to over 20 magazines."

Later, I decided that his interest in "everything" was one key to his health and longevity. But in that interview I wanted to get his ideas about how he had managed to stay healthy.

"Do you think your diet helped you to stay healthy and reach this age?" I asked.

"Well," replied Ralph, "my mother taught me to eat good foods. And, although it might seem silly to you, she always said, 'Don't eat too fast. Chew your food well. That way you can digest it well and benefit from the food's nutrition.' Now, chewing well is more important to me than ever. I think today's emphasis on fast foods, eaten fast, is a great health problem. I have always liked healthy foods, such as seafood and vegetables and fruit."

His voice was clear and strong and his blue eyes twinkled as he spoke. He laughed when I said, "A friend of mine says she is a 'chocoholic, a junk food junkie and a fast-food freak.' Maybe we should all listen to your mother."

"Has your voice always been strong?" I asked. "Many

people your age seem to have weak voices."

"Teaching classes in botany at Gordon College in Pakistan for 50 years helped to strengthen my voice," said he. "And, while working in the University of Michigan Herbarium for 21 years after retirement I kept my voice strong by singing in my local church choir. As you may know, I continued to sing in our Westminster Gardens retirement community choir here until I was 93 years old. All that kept my voice strong."

"What about exercise?" I asked.

"I have been active all my life," replied Ralph. "As a student at Columbia University in New York I won three gold medals for running on the relay team and also medals for wrestling. At Gordon College I joined our students in playing tennis, soccer and basketball. Hiking the Himalayan hills and mountains to collect plants for my botany collection also helped. Even now, at age 102, I exercise. After sitting for 50 minutes I get up and walk the nursing home halls for ten minutes – all day long."

Saying this, he walked unaided over to his walker and added, "Sometimes I go outside to pick flowers. I went to the swimming pool for daily swims until I was 101." At the pool I had seen him hold his nose and jump in with a big splash. I was always relieved to see him come up again.

"What role has heredity played in your staying healthy at this age?" I asked.

"As someone has said, I did 'choose the right parents,'" he replied. "My father lived to be 88 and my mother to be 90. That was unusual in their day. I am sure my good genes helped. But that is not enough; my brother died at age 75. I think it was because he retired and had no real purpose for living. Keeping up my botany research and my interest in politics and the environment help keep me healthy. I also still keep up my stamp collecting hobby."

Regarding his activities, I knew what he was talking about. I was his assistant in writing a book on the trees, shrubs and vines in Westminster Gardens when he wrote it at age 95. A 60-page book, it has received professional praise. However, it is not equal to his scientific tome, *An Annotated Catalogue of the Plants of Pakistan and Kashmir,* which is a 1,005-page book weighing five pounds – written when he was only 82. Having a purpose in life during retirement has certainly helped to give him a positive outlook on life which, I think, has contributed to his health.

"If you had to give one main reason why you are still healthy at age 102, what would it be?" I asked.

"Well, I would have to say that I believe it is because God had something for me to do even in my old age," replied Ralph. "I do believe that it is a Higher Power that guides and controls our lives, including our health and age. Others may not agree, but that is my belief."

Knowing I couldn't argue with that, I got up to leave. As I was going out Ralph called out, "Come back again if you think of other questions. I will try to answer them – if I can remember. One reason I have to stay in this nursing home is that I can remember things from long ago, but not recent things. I can remember what my red-brick school looked like in first grade. But don't ask me what I had for breakfast!" And he laughed. "If you want to know all the facts, see my daughter, Ellen."

Ah! That's another reason for his health, I thought. He has kept his sense of humor. Dr. Ralph Stewart has certainly set a good example for us.

His faithfulness in serving his neighbor has been recognized by many officials. In 1938 he received a medal from the British king for his educational work in India. In 1962 the Pakistan government honored him for his educational work there and on his 100th birthday, the Pakistan government invited him and his daughter Ellen – and paid all their expenses – to celebrate his birthday there. It was a way to thank him for bequeathing to the Pakistanis his entire botany collection.

So, according to Ralph, to be healthy at 102 we need to eat good food, chew well, stay active, keep a positive outlook and a sense of humor, maintain wide interests, have the right genes and continue to be useful to God and to those around us.

42

Serving Retired Missionaries

Miguel Gomez-Aguirre, better known as "Mike," has served retired missionaries and ministers at Westminster Gardens in California longer than any other employee – 37 years of dedicated Christian service.

"When I first came here in 1956," said Mike, "this small town of Duarte was mostly a farming area. Often I saw coyotes, raccoons, and even deer, wandering around among the fruit trees of our campus. As recently as ten years ago a mother coyote gave birth to her pups here on our grounds."

Mike is a Mexican Tarascan Indian who grew up in the Indian village of Numeron, in Michoacan, Mexico—about 300 miles southwest of Mexico City. "My father owned a butcher shop," said Mike, "but he died when I was ten, so from then on I helped my mother operate the shop. The butcher shop did not make much money and I knew that someday my mother would be too weak to work there. In a few years I began dreaming about getting a job in the U.S. where I could earn more money and take better care of my mother.

"I started working on my application papers when I was still 15. Suddenly I got a chance to go to the U.S. when some relatives there invited my aunt to visit them in Azusa, California. She kindly let me come along—with the idea I would stay if I found a job. We arrived in August of 1955 and soon I found a job in Azusa picking avocados. Every month I sent money home to my mother in Mexico. I took care of her financially for the rest of her life."

"After two years of picking fruit and working part-time at Westminster Gardens, I was offered a full-time post in May, 1957. I have never considered working anywhere else. I feel very much at home here. Although my main job was the gardening, I was called upon to do many jobs—from helping to carry patients up and down stairs before they installed elevators to working a bucket brigade during a flash flood."

Soon after starting work at Westminster Gardens, Mike met and married a lovely Mexican-American girl from nearby Azusa. Soon they were on their way to raising a family of six children.

When he first began work at Westminster Gardens, Mike's boss was a man named Joe whom Mike liked but who sometimes, Mike felt, used poor judgment. One day he had to do a job that required climbing up on a high ladder. Mike tried to put the ladder where he thought best, but Joe insisted, "No, put the ladder over here."

It didn't look too safe to Mike, but wanting to please Joe, he took his advice and climbed up the ladder. In the middle of his chore the ladder suddenly gave way and Mike fell, hitting his knee on a rock. For two weeks he couldn't even walk, but soon Mike was back on the job, working hard and cheerfully again. When Mike became gardening supervisor, he resolved to be very careful where he told his gardening crew to put their ladders.

And he has always tried to protect his crew. A Westminster resident recalls, "Once a large sycamore tree beside my house had to be trimmed because it was leaning over the roof and might fall in a storm. Since it was precarious already, no one wanted to climb up to do the job. Suddenly, I saw Supervisor Mike up there trimming away – while his crew half his age stood looking on!"

Another resident said, "Not long ago we almost lost Mike. He was lowering some pumping equipment into the swimming pool to empty it for winter. Unknown to Mike, the equipment had an electrical short in it. When it hit the water Mike received a horrible shock. The only thing that saved him was that someone quickly pulled the electric plug, shutting off the electricity."

Later Mike admitted, "After that shock I had to run around the pool about ten times before I started to feel normal again." The next day Mike was back on the job, working as if nothing had happened.

During his 37 years of service at Westminster Gardens, Mike has developed the lawns, flower gardens, fruit trees and flowering shrubs to the point where Westminster Gardens is really deserving of the name "Gardens." With careful planning,

171

Mike has something in bloom all twelve months of the year. Visitors "ooh and aah" as they tour the Gardens.

Mike never was able to complete his education beyond the sixth grade. He still can't speak English as well as he would like, but in his service to the 200 residents of the Gardens, Mike speaks another language very well – the language of Christian love and faithful service. Recently he began weekly English classes – at age 60.

Although Mike was never able to get the education he wanted, he made sure that his four boys and two girls all graduated from high school. And, with a little help from a former director of the gardens, Mike's son, Mike Jr., graduated from junior college and is now a skilled electrical technician – in charge of the street lights and other electrical work for the city of Azusa. Another son, Richard, is supervisor of all the parks and garden work of the city of Azusa. All of Mike's children have turned out well and in the process have produced ten grandchildren for Mike and his wife.

Although his six children are U.S. citizens, Mike has never had time to become one himself. But, unlike the "wetbacks," Mike has never been here illegally. It took him ten years to work out all the papers and arrangements, but he came in legally in 1955, and has remained legal ever since – and has his original "green card" to prove it.

Mike owns his own home now and plans to retire near Westminster Gardens, but first he plans to keep Westminster Gardens looking beautiful for another five years.

Recently a friend asked Mike, "Why do you keep working with all those *old* people?" Mike replied, "You and I will be old someday. What's wrong with working for old people?" The residents at the Gardens certainly appreciate all he does to make their life beautiful.

43

Grandpa Ed and Grandma Kate Carwile

My Christian Grandpa

I remember Grandpa Carwile as a tall, lanky man with a gray mustache. A few times I had the good fortune to join him in work on his farm, during which I would trot along behind him trying to keep up.

On the farm it was the custom to have dinner in the middle of the day and then take a nap before going back to the fields. I will always remember Grandpa resting on the porch or on the grass under a tree in the yard with his gray mustache fluttering delightfully in the breeze as he snored away.

Grandpa liked sweets. Often he would take a "snack break" of a handful of brown sugar – which he always carefully shared with me. Another favorite snack was sweet potatoes which Grandma Kate often had on the stove. Grandpa loved to tell the story about his son-in-law, Charlie Farris, when he was courting their daughter, Mag. Apparently Grandma Kate was just taking a batch of sweet potatoes from the oven when Charlie came into the kitchen. She said, "Charlie, would you like to have a sweet potato?" Charlie's quick response was, "I had rather have Mag!" Early I learned that brides are more attractive than sweet potatoes.

Our family reunions of the Carwile-Hendricks-Driskill families were usually held at Grandpa Carwile's farm. Every time I went I met relatives I didn't know I had. At one of those picnics I saw Grandpa mediate a quarrel between two of his grown daughters. I was deeply impressed by his sensitive, loving Christian spirit, for somehow he managed to make peace between them without taking sides and without hurting the feelings of either one. Although small at the time, I knew that Grandpa had a fine Christian spirit which I would like to have. Later, as I heard him teaching a Sunday school class, I learned where he got that loving Christian spirit.

That spirit was shown in the unselfish way he supported his children and their families, sometimes at great sacrifice to himself, even to the loss of his farm. No wonder a daughter-in-law was heard to say, "He was the finest Christian man I have ever known." I admired Grandpa Carwile so much that I named our son Edward after him. Strangely, he turned out to be left-handed – just like his great-grandpa, Ed Carwile, was.

44

A World of Joy and Wonder

When I was seven, I was shut up in a dark room with a discouraging illness that lasted several weeks. I felt lonely and depressed, shut off from my family and the outside world. Finally, I got well enough to go outside.

As I opened the living room door, I saw a thrilling sight. The whole hillside beyond our yard was covered with a blaze of white and pink apple blossoms. I was speechless. It seemed as though God was saying to me, "Welcome back to the world of health, joy and wonder!"

That glorious scene became permanently fixed in my memory as are other wonderful experiences I have had down through the years. One winter day I woke to find the whole world around me made clean and white by a new snowfall.

Admiring it from a window, I was thrilled to see a flock of "snowbirds" (Juncos) suddenly descend from the sky – small gray dots on the blanket of white. I watched as they busily scratched down through the snow to find the hidden grass seeds below. They looked like animated raisins hopping happily about on the top of a huge cake with white frosting. I remembered what Jesus had said about God taking care of the "birds of the air."

Another scene etched on my memory happened one night when I was ten, sitting on the grass in our yard admiring the millions of bright stars in the sky above me. Suddenly I wondered what was really up there. Were there other planets up there with other little boys just like me? While I mused there that night my friendly dog Brownie came and sat down beside me, leaning his warm body against my side. Suddenly I was filled with joy. The combination of a starry sky and my loving dog triggered deep feelings of wonder in me. "How are all these things related? God made them all, so certainly there is some relationship that God will reveal to me someday." I am still wondering – but with joy in my wonder.

A few years later I heard that beavers, which we all thought had become extinct in our area, had made a comeback near my home in Virginia. At the first opportunity, I went to see the new beaver pond and sat quietly on the bank as the daylight faded into twilight – the time beavers sometimes come out to work on their dam. Imagine my thrill of joy when a large beaver came gliding through the water. All I could see were his eyes, nose and part of his back, as he swam toward me. Working silently and swiftly, he began repairing a weak place in the dam, using sticks and mud.

Silently I watched enthralled, not daring to move for fear he would be scared away. I lost track of time. Closing my eyes,

I could imagine early American Indians sitting where I sat, watching a similar scene and I felt at peace with God's creatures, both animal and human. When I finally had to move my cramped legs, the beaver slapped his tail sharply against the water—and disappeared. I remained there transfixed, reluctant to have this thrilling experience end. But it didn't end, for I can still see it and feel it, years later, as part of my treasured "memory bank."

Probably the most deeply felt experience of my life was the thrill of holding my newborn son in my arms for the first time. After hours of anxious waiting—during a long and difficult birth—I saw the doctor suddenly appear in the waiting room doorway. "Would you like to hold your new baby son for a moment?"

Would I! My heart jumping with joy, I cradled the warm bundle in my arms. Thrills ran through me like electric shocks. Filled with gratitude to God I prayed, "Thank you, God, for the gift of this wonderful new baby. Thank you for letting us share in this creation of a new life."

This sense of joy and gratitude was repeated, in a different way, when our baby girl arrived two years later. The fact that we almost lost her because of a strange blood problem threatened to plunge us into despair. But a miraculous blood transfusion, when she was only one week old, saved her life. Seeing her snap back to life, I again prayed a joyful prayer, "Thank you, God, for snatching our little baby back from the brink of death." Again, my heart almost burst with joy and gratitude. I had discovered that joy can seem deeper and greater when felt in contrast to the sorrow and pain that has preceded it.

What do all of these experiences of joy and wonder have in common? They are all "peak experiences" which have met some mysterious spiritual and psychological need within me.

They are so vivid in my memory that I can recall them and enjoy them, again and again – all through my life. I also think that God's gift of such experiences helped me to avoid getting hooked on artificial "highs" of drugs, nicotine or alcohol. I didn't need such artificial "highs" because God had already given me the real thing, a *natural* sense of joy and wonder.

What about you? Developing your own sense of joy and wonder could help you overcome the temptation to try artificial, chemically induced "highs." Natural "peak experiences" are a vital part of the "abundant life" Christ has promised to give us. Why settle for anything less?

About the Author

Born in Virginia, Dr. J. Lawrence Driskill and his family served as missionaries to Japan for over two decades. A graduate of Penn State University, Princeton Seminary and San Francisco Theological Seminary, he wrote his doctoral dissertation on a study of evangelism in Japan's Senri Newtown – a huge housing complex for 150,000 new residents. After leaving Japan, Dr. Driskill has served churches in Texas, Tennessee and California. Presently he lives in Duarte, California and continues to assist Japanese-American congregations in the Los Angeles area, preaching in both English and Japanese.

Additional copies of this book may be obtained
from your local bookstore,
or by sending $11.95 per paperback copy, postpaid,
$19.95 per library hardcover copy, postpaid,
to:

Hope Publishing House
P.O. Box 60008
Pasadena, CA 91116

CA residents add 8¼% sales tax
FAX orders to: (818) 792-2121
Telephone VISA/MC orders to: (800) 326-2671